THE
PICNIC

THE PICNIC

Recipes *and* Inspiration *from* Basket *to* Blanket

MARNIE HANEL, ANDREA SLONECKER & JEN STEVENSON

Illustrations by Emily Isabella

ARTISAN
NEW YORK

Library of Congress Cataloging-in-Publication Data

Hanel, Marnie, author.
The picnic : recipes and inspiration from basket to blanket /
Marnie Hanel, Andrea Slonecker, and Jen Stevenson.
pages cm
Includes an index.
ISBN 978-1-57965-608-9
1. Picnics. I. Slonecker, Andrea, author. II. Stevenson, Jen, 1977– author.
III. Title.
TX823.H33 2014
642'.3–dc23 2014036496

Design by Renata Di Biase

Artisan books are available at special discounts when purchased in bulk for premiums and sales promotions as well as for fund-raising or educational use. Special editions or book excerpts also can be created to specifications. For details, contact the Special Sales Director at the address below, or send an e-mail to specialmarkets@workman.com.

Published by Artisan
A division of Workman Publishing Company, Inc.
225 Varick Street
New York, NY 10014-4381
artisanbooks.com

Published simultaneously in Canada by Thomas Allen & Son, Limited.

Printed in China
First printing, April 2015

10 9 8 7 6 5 4 3 2 1

For
the Portland Picnic Society

Contents

Ball
MASON

Preface

AT THE FIRST SIGN OF SPRING, when the crocus blossoms peek through the grass and the bluebirds return to the trees, we start dreaming of picnic season—a celebration that kicks off the first warm day of the year and lingers through crisp early fall. Our first picnic might only involve grabbing a sandwich and a paperback and heading to the park for a quick lunch, but as the days get longer, our picnics become more and more elaborate—lending themselves to date nights, outdoor concerts, movie screenings, plays, book clubs, campouts, birthdays, baby showers, engagement parties, brunches, and beach parties.

We love picnicking so much that we decided to make a habit of it. Four years ago, we walked to our favorite park, found a perfectly situated picnic table, spread a tablecloth, and unpacked rounds of molten-centered triple crème, bowls of sweet Shuksan strawberries, tiny pots of lemon curd topped with soft spoonfuls of whipped cream, and (perhaps most important) a wine cellar's worth of rosé. One by one, our friends appeared, bearing the makings of an alfresco feast. Once the spread was suitably sumptuous, we filled our plates with deviled eggs and dilly beans, asparagus salad and fresh cherries tossed with mint, little leek tarts and slices of poached salmon, and we settled onto our blankets for a meal that lasted late into the night. Needless to say, we were hooked, completely taken with the ease and spontaneity of our get-together. Only a few hours passed before we started planning the next one, and it wasn't long before it became a monthly affair. And so the Portland Picnic Society was formed, quite by accident.

Picnics are a silver bullet for summer entertaining—they take the stress out of parties and leave only the fun. For the modern hostess, whose friends often outnumber her chair count, bringing the party to the park makes it possible to gather any number of people, with less effort than it takes to find a restaurant to accommodate a large group. Picnics require far less fuss than hosting a party at home, too, since you can forget about cleaning the house or washing a single dish. And because the menu expands and contracts with the guest count, there's no need to worry about last-minute additions or cancellations. Invite just a few friends, or catch up with all of your favorite companions in one fell swoop—there's always enough food at a picnic, since everyone pitches in.

Beyond being a great way to gather, picnics offer an excellent framework for exploring new recipes. Whether you have ten minutes to make a snappy snack or an afternoon set aside for a series of summery projects—pickles, paletas, or Mason jar pies—you'll find many ways to wow. And since nothing impresses us more than a picnic of the Hyde Park variety, at which a glance at a nearby blanket might yield a magnum of Champagne, an entire roast chicken, and a three-tier cake, we hope you'll delight in a sampling of foods you might not have previously considered bringing to the park.

These recipes are tried and tested, but we hope you'll play with them, making the most of seasonal ingredients, snipping herbs from your window garden, and riffling through your bar cart for splashes of substitutions. Our picnics aspire to the same level of detail, creativity, and charm as if we were entertaining in our own homes—in essence, we're just kicking off our flats and taking the party outdoors—and we hope you'll do the same. Besides, we like the challenge of planning a meal that's somehow even better without the comforts of a kitchen.

Remember to check the basket packing list to make sure you have everything you need—you'll find one at the end of each recipe—or prepare to improvise with the contents of your handbag. That's just the kind of creativity that makes these recipes our go-to picks. Speaking of which, go forth and picnic! And be sure to show off your delicacies as you do. Join us online at #thepicnicbook.

Xo,
Marnie, Andrea, and Jen

CHAPTER 1

From Basket to Blanket

These are a few of the critical skills that separate the picnic novice from the picnic pro, and with the help of this definitive picnic primer, you'll be the latter in the time it takes to spread a Pendleton blanket in the Champ de Mars. These pages will take you from picnic planning to pack-up, supplying you with the definitive picnic packing list, setting forth pivotal picnic standards and practices, and even schooling you in the art of choosing the perfect picnic site. So read on, preferably while sitting in your favorite park, for an advanced education in picnicking.

Pop-Up Picnic

In its most basic form, a relaxing picnic requires nothing more than stepping outside with a few nibbles. When a languid morning turns into a peckish afternoon—or when the weather is fair and the boss is out of the office—head for the hills with a picnic of store-bought provisions. Here are some ideas for a modern twist on the ploughman's lunch.

Farmers' Market

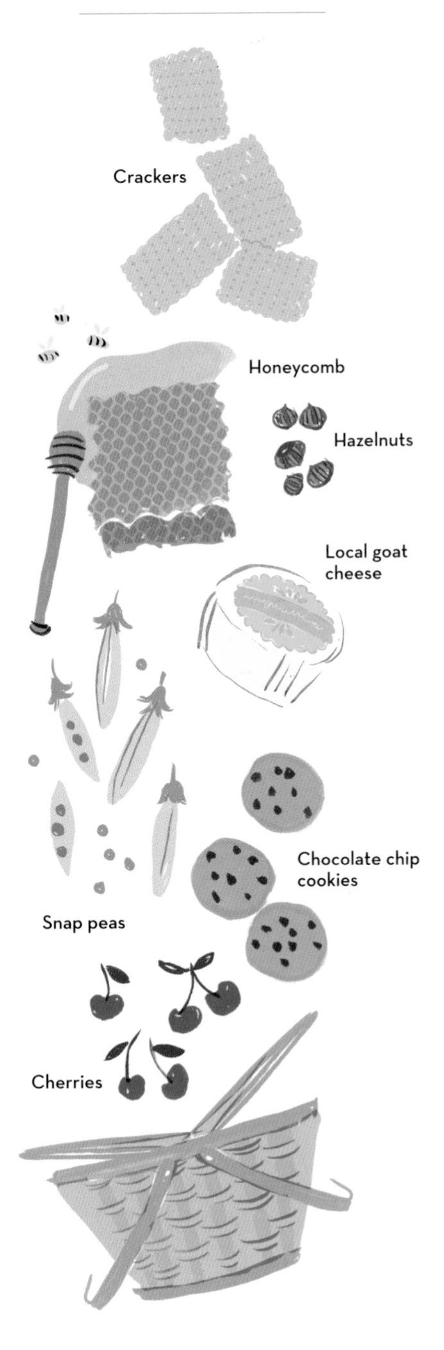

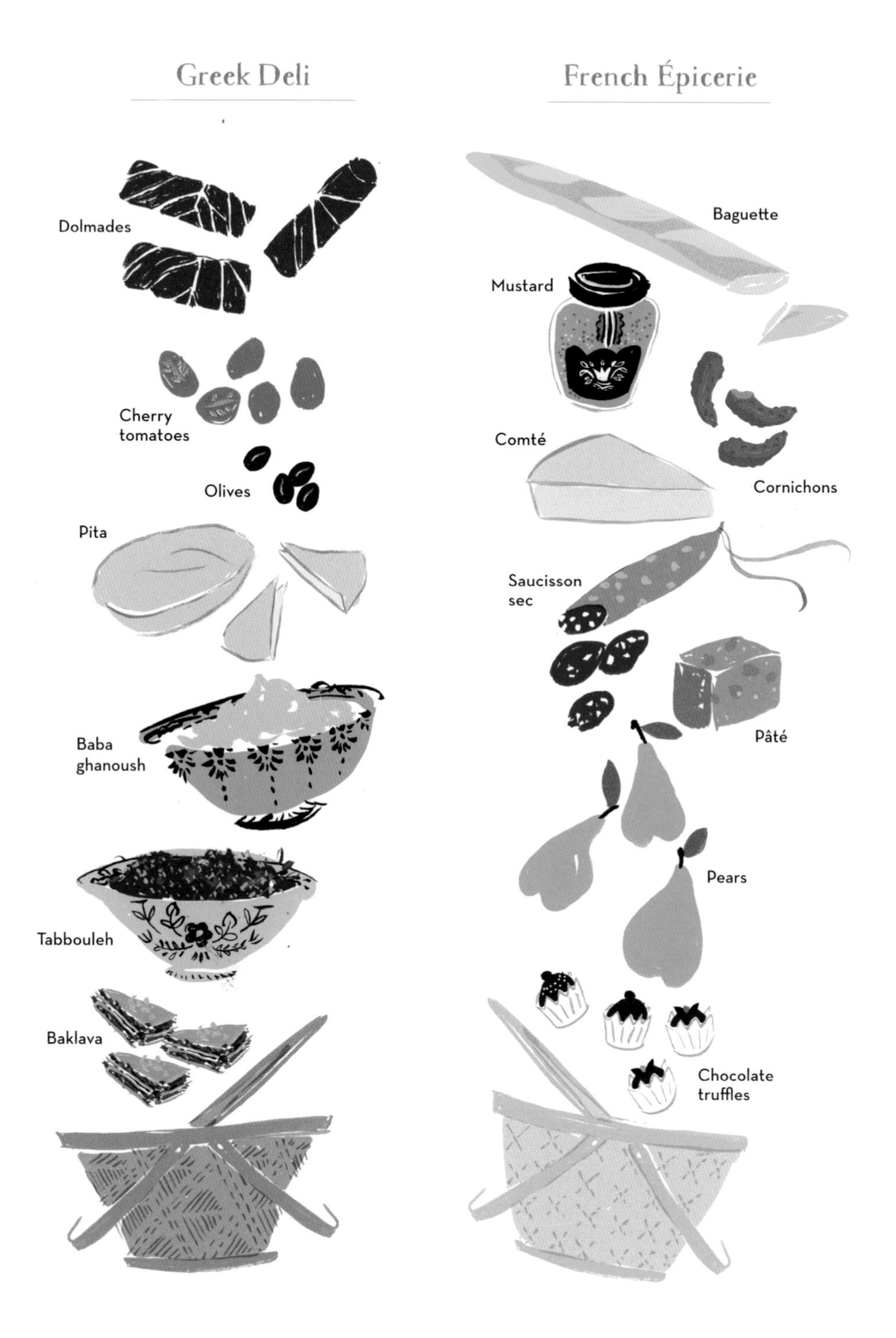
Greek Deli
Dolmades
Cherry tomatoes
Olives
Pita
Baba ghanoush
Tabbouleh
Baklava
French Épicerie
Baguette
Mustard
Comté
Cornichons
Saucisson sec
Pâté
Pears
Chocolate truffles

Picnic Party Primer

Even the most spontaneous of parties have an invisible hand behind them, making sure all picnickers find the picnic site easily and have something to drink and eat when they get there. Here's how to pull off a picnic that's just the right mix of ease and enchantment.

❶ Menu Planning

Unless you have an incredibly telepathic group of friends, it's a good idea to ask everyone to declare what they're bringing in advance via a round-robin email. Otherwise you might end up with twenty chicken salads and zero desserts. Choose a theme to inspire the masses. (For ideas, see the menus on pages 51, 55, 72, 78, 102, 113, 131, 154, 155, and 174.)

❷ Portioning

Break out this reference chart to calculate the appropriate number of items to bring. If guests need direction, assign bites, salads, plates, sweets, and sips. Most of the recipes in this book serve four to six people.

GUESTS	BITES	SALADS	PLATES	SWEETS	SIPS
2 people	Optional	1	1	1	1
4-6 people	1	2	1	1	1
8-12 people	2	3	2	2	2
14-20 people	3	4	3	3	3

❸ Keep It Real

There's a plethora of dishware designed to be tossed after outdoor use, but if you picnic often, it's worth procuring a set of inexpensive silverware and durable plates (think: melamine, tin, or enamel). It's always nice to be sweet to Mother Earth—after all, she's hosting the party.

❹ Oh, Fork

If you happen to have plates, glasses, and utensils for your entire picnic group, tell your guests that you'll provide them. But if you do not, tell your guests *exactly* what they're expected to bring to the blanket. Tote a few extra place settings for drop-in (or forgetful) picnickers.

❺ Arrive Ahead

Be sure to get to the picnic site at least thirty minutes before the rest of the group to stake your claim on the perfect picnic table or parcel of grass.

❻ Get the Digits

Once you've chosen a picnic site, text message a drop pin of your location to the other guests. Detailed descriptions of adjacent landmarks—nearest park entrance, statue of your city's founder, tightrope walkers—also prove very useful.

❼ Retreat and Repeat

When the dining is done, divvy up the leftovers, pack up the trash and dishes, set the date for the next picnic, and stroll home, satiated and satisfied.

TINY TIP

A standard-size picnic table is 2½ by 8 feet (30 by 96 inches), so make sure your tablecloth is at least 108 inches long.

Scout Your Spot

Besides the food, the number one factor in an idyllic picnic is location, location, location. Here's a complete list to evaluate each component of your setting. Check all of the boxes, and congratulations—you're ready to picnic in comfort!

Topography

- ☐ Lush, green grass
- ☐ No hidden swamp pits
- ☐ Free of beehives, ant colonies, and wasp nests
- ☐ Level terrain, devoid of large divots and hidden sharp objects
- ☐ Scenic views (e.g., rose garden, meadow, forest clearing, bodies of water)

Amenities

- ☐ Appropriate distance from bathrooms
- ☐ Adequate parking within schlepping distance
- ☐ Trash and recycle bins nearby (but not too close)
- ☐ Picnic table (optional)

Not Within 100 Feet of Site

- ☐ Blaring boom boxes
- ☐ Large flocks of seagulls
- ☐ Freeway
- ☐ Naked bike-ride registrants
- ☐ Parked ice cream truck playing a jingle on a loop

Blanket Buying Guide

When selecting your picnic blanket, look for these qualities. For ideas about where to shop for the best blankets, see Picnic Provisions (page 185).

Washable: Every picnic involves a certain degree of carnage—spilled wine, squished deviled eggs, dirt—which is why spreads that you can toss directly into the laundry are perfect picnic blankets. Look for cotton throws, Turkish towels, tablecloths, and large swaths of fabric for lightweight, laundry-safe options.

Waterproof: Blankets with waterproof backing may be more difficult to clean, but after summer rains, they're a great pick for the park.

Old: Repurpose a retired quilt. But save yourself from the unpleasant realization that grass dew leads to mildew. After the picnic, air out your quilt on the porch, or over your shower-curtain rod, to dry it completely before folding it back up and tucking it away.

Extra: For outdoor concerts, movies, and Shakespeare in the Park, bring additional throw blankets, wraps, and even pillows to pile upon the picnic blanket.

TINY TIP

How big should your blanket be? As a rule of thumb, calculate at least 9 square feet of space per picnicker for a comfortable seating arrangement (i.e., a 5-by-7-foot blanket is suitable for three, but a little tight for four).

From Kitchen to Basket

Stylish and sweet baskets are the darlings of picnic portability. But inside every prodigious tote is a pack of petite helpers. Here are the unsung heroes of food transportation, necessities for any alfresco adventurer.

Good Ol' Tupperware

There's a reason people throw parties for these lidded carryalls—they changed food transportation forever. Use Tupperware (or your favorite brand of portable container) to bring fragile cookies, juicy salads, and multi-component main dishes to the park. When you arrive at the park, re-plate your dish on a platter or cake plate to elevate it from workaday fare to a special-occasion marvel.

Mason, Weck, and Le Parfait Jars

Show off summer dishes by carrying, displaying, and even eating them in a glass jar. Mr. Mason is easy to find *and* easy on your pocketbook, while the wondrous Weck jar adds industrial flair in an inspiring variety of shapes and sizes. The hinge-top closure of a French Le Parfait jar is très chic for pâtés and pickles, and you'll never lose the lid. See page 24 for myriad ways to use jars, and Picnic Provisions (page 185) for sources.

Pyrex

Take advantage of the depth (and handles) of an everyday 9-by-13-inch glass baking dish to transport prearranged bites that need a bit of headspace. (Here's looking at you, Salads on a Stick, page 76.) Cover tightly with plastic wrap for the kitchen-to-picnic trek, then simply unwrap and serve.

Baking Pans

Rather than risk squishing your sweets, take them from the oven to the picnic in the container they were baked in—be that a muffin tin, a springform cake pan, or a loaf pan. At the picnic, remove the baked goods from the pan and arrange them on a platter.

Tiffins

India's high-rise lunch pails pack goodies in stacked layers, so they're nicely suited for separating items better left unacquainted. Pack the Ooh-La-La Niçoise (page 70) tiffin-style, or break down an array of appetizers into four layers—say, Shocking-Pink Beet Hummus (page 58), olives, cheese, and crackers. You can also create a compact cooling system by filling the bottom tier of the tiffin with ice and packing the layers above with items that require a little headspace, like the Deviled Dozen (page 36).

Bento Boxes

For the rare picnic at which you're preparing *all* the food, pre-portion each meal in a bento box, which offers opportunities for artfully arranging colorful dishes of any provenance. For planning ideas, see the Oh My, Omakase menu on page 55. Have fun with the tiny compartments, tucking surprises (wrapped rice candy, origami fortune-tellers, teensy bottles of soy sauce) into each. Wrap the boxes tightly with plastic wrap and serve at the picnic with chopsticks.

Tips & Tricks:
Tools

You might not have considered bringing the following household items to a picnic, but here's why you should.

For obvious reasons. And because the other picnickers forgot theirs.

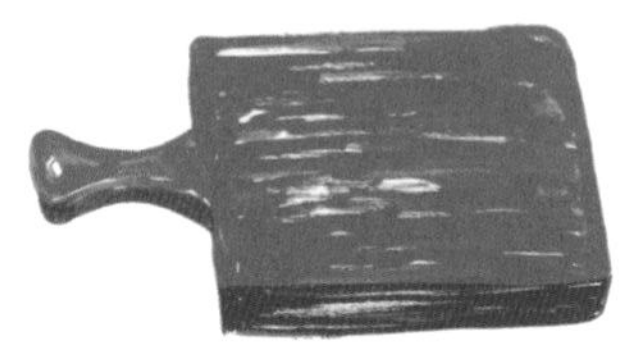

Chop fresh herbs and cut lemon wedges, or set up a cheese or charcuterie board.

For deviled eggs, bring the filling in a resealable plastic bag and the egg whites in a container. At the park, snip the corner of the bag and pipe in the filling.

Slice through everything from a sandwich to a galette.

Whip cream and dress delicate greens on-site.

Carry a common condiments kit (CCK): salt, pepper, olive oil, and lemon.

The Ultimate Basket:
A Picnic Bike

Zip up to your picnic in this customized bicycle, which stores everything you need in a built-in carrying case. So far, this lives only in our dreams, but please let us know when it's available for sale. We'll be the first in line.

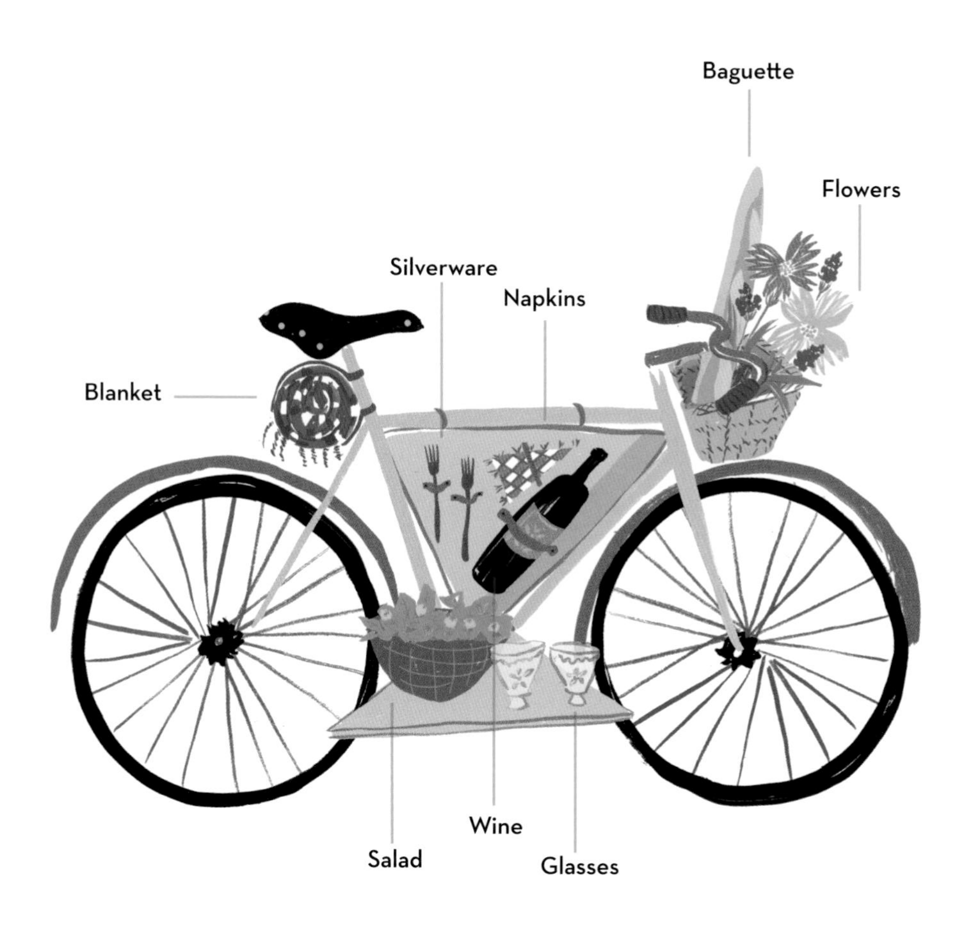

Practical Porters

In an ideal world, all of your food and supplies would fit into a single basket, but sometimes your picnic goodies need special accommodations. Here are some alternatives that have been proven to work as never intended.

Galvanized Tin Pails • These lightweight gardening go-tos make excellent improvised ice buckets, flower vases, utensil caddies, or trash cans.

Stockpot • You can actually cart a dozen whole, steamed crabs in a stockpot. Or pounds upon pounds of ice. It's heavy, but boy, is it big.

Laundry Basket • Designed to hold at least two weeks' worth of clothing, a laundry basket also has the capacity to carry plates, cutlery, and napkins for twelve, crostini with toppings, a full-size salad bowl with servers, a roast chicken, and a carving board.

Canvas Tote • Not quite as quintessential as a proper picnic basket, these practical totes are the hauling heroes of an outdoor gathering, and you can wash the spilt Strawberry Shrub Sparkler (page 165) right out of them.

Radio Flyer • Whimsical and practical, a little red wagon is to a park what a rolling suitcase is to an airplane.

Chinatown Shopping Cart • The urban grocery tote gets a sylvan spin when stuffed to the brim with picnic supplies. Pack heavy items (e.g., serveware) on the bottom and delicacies (e.g., strawberries) on the top.

Wheelie Coolers • The trolley dolly of a prepared picnicker, coolers on wheels are the beverage taxi of choice for outdoor gatherings. Keep yours even colder with a double layer of ice: place a 5-pound brick of dry ice at the bottom of the cooler and empty a bag of party ice on top of it.

From Bar to Blanket

Take it easy and pick up bottles of bubbles for your picnic, or use these purpose-built sipper schleppers for homemade libations.

Stoppered Bottle

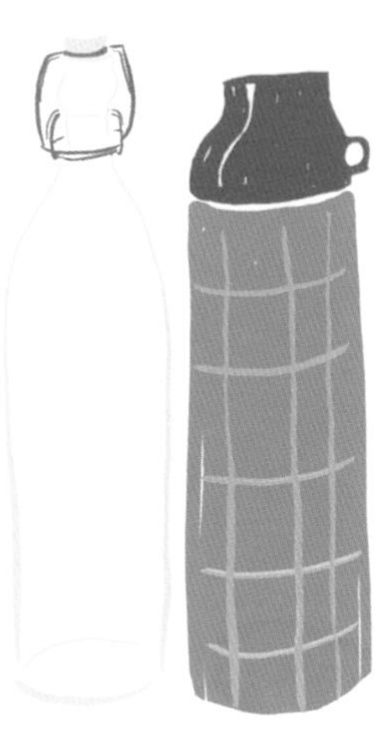

Use a funnel to pour lemonade, or even a batch of cocktails, into a 1-liter glass bottle with a rubber stopper. Purchase your favorite French lemonade and recycle the bottle, or buy these separately at the specialty retailers listed in Picnic Provisions (page 185).

Thermos

While traditionally celebrated for its ability to keep cocoa hot, a thermos is equally useful for keeping drinks cold. So, dust off the Stanley from your camping box, fill it with ice cubes and iced tea, and serve up an arctic refreshment.

Champagne Splits

These little sippers make a big impression. Pre-bottle cocktails at home using single-portion 187-ml Champagne bottles and a bottle capper (see page 164).

Drink Dispenser

A glass beverage container is worth its weight in drips and spills, so consider corralling your iced tea and agua fresca in a proper drink dispenser with a spigot. At two or more gallons, it's a practical solution for large gatherings, but be sure to pack the Radio Flyer for the haul.

99 Ways (and Counting) to Use a Mason Jar

1. Utensil caddy
2. Straw dispenser
3. Cocktail shaker
4. Vase
5. Firefly catcher
6. Oil lamp
7. Dip dish
8. Pudding dish
9. Place card holder
10. Candy jar
11. Rolling pin
12. Powdered sugar shaker
13. Layered salad container
14. Popsicle mold
15. Charades clues holder
16. Shot glass
17. Whipped cream shaker
18. Personal pie dish
19. Lantern
20. Badminton boundary markers
21. Harmonica case
22. Scorecard holder
23. Soup bowl
24. Ice cream dish
25. Ice cream scoop rest
26. Bones bin
27. Pit depository
28. Oyster shell collector
29. Herb planter
30. Toothpick holder
31. Napkin holder
32. Balloon weight
33. Moist towelette holder
34. Blanket weight
35. Cupcake holder
36. Message in a bottle bottle
37. Fruit bowl
38. Olive oil jar
39. Moonshine distillery
40. Soda float glass
41. Spin the Bottle bottle
42. Key collector
43. Olive dish
44. Beverage dispenser
45. Cheese dome
46. Sunglass case
47. Cookie jar
48. Water glass
49. Jell-O mold
50. Breadstick holder
51. Fermentation crock
52. Cookie cutter
53. Condiment set
54. Twine dispenser
55. Dressing drizzler
56. Garnish keeper
57. Crudité holder
58. Votive holder

59. Butter keeper
60. Saltcellar
61. First-aid kit holder
62. Matchbox (with sandpaper-lined lid)
63. Drum kit
64. Ring holder
65. Mortar
66. Punch bowl
67. Wineglass
68. Beer stein
69. Collection jar
70. Measuring cup
71. Sidewalk chalk carrier
72. Spice shaker
73. Caviar cooler
74. Hummingbird bath
75. Nut jar
76. Compost collector
77. Pesto saver
78. Lemon wedge holder
79. Citrus zest keeper
80. Pitcher
81. Vinaigrette shaker
82. Time capsule
83. Citronella candle pot
84. Popcorn holder
85. Teapot
86. Coffee cup
87. Maraca
88. Petty cash dispenser
89. Ice scooper
90. Dice cup
91. Takeout container
92. Chopstick holder
93. Egg poacher
94. Beer Pong glass
95. Pickle jar
96. Jelly jar
97. Tip jar
98. Lost and found jar
99. Small hat

Darling, Disaster!
Ten Picnic Crises Averted

Sometimes even the most well-planned party goes pear-shaped. Picnic problem-free with this guide to outwitting catastrophes.

❶ Permits, Please

Picnics thrive on spontaneity, but it can be a good idea to ask for permission. If you're gathering a large group in a public park, apply for a permit through your city's Department of Parks and Recreation. You can book a baseball diamond or bocce court for an after-meal activity. And if your athleticism is limited to lifting your picnic basket, many parks will allow you to purchase an alcohol permit, too.

❷ Cop Stop

On the off chance you forgot to get a permit for alcohol consumption, be sure to sip discreetly. Premix your cocktails in bottles, avoid drinking out of stemware, and, should those methods fail, offer the friendly officer a sincere apology and a bite to eat. Just make sure it's not the Chicken Liver Mousse with Lillet Gelée (page 56).

❸ In Case of Rain

On picnic's eve: Should a summer thunderstorm render your picnic site soggy, implore your friends to tote their yoga mats to the park—unfurl them on the lawn and cover them with the blanket to keep bottoms dry. Or buy a vinyl tablecloth or camping tarp to tuck beneath your blanket.

On picnic day: Relocate to a covered outdoor space: a gazebo, picnic shelter, yurt, tepee, or enormous tent. If all else fails, head for the living room.

During the picnic: Drop that lightning-loving metal fork, grab the food, and run for cover.

❹ Bathroom Break

Nothing ruins a picnic like having to go, with no relief in sight. Scout the state of your picnic site's restrooms upon arrival. If they're locked or loathsome, search for the nearest coffeehouse and inform your friends of its location.

❺ First-Aid Fortifications

When badminton rackets and croquet mallets start flying, anything can happen. Fill a resealable bag with Band-Aids, aspirin, tampons, sunscreen, anti-itch cream, dental floss, antacids, an EpiPen, and $20 in case the ice cream man scoots past in his truck.

❻ Beat the Heat

If it's a real sizzler of a day, surprise your fellow guests with a Mediterranean-scented cooldown: add a few drops of rose, citrus, or lavender oil to chilled miniature spray bottles of water and distribute them to the crowd. (Paper fans work, too.)

❼ All Choked Up

In the rare, unfortunate case of a quail-egg-clogged esophagus, use the following protocol: Ask, "Are you choking, or are you joking?" Then command the victim to stand and thump him squarely between his shoulder blades; clasp him around his midsection, make a fist and place your other hand over it, and thrust suddenly. The offending article should present itself.

❽ Pernicious Plants

Should you find yourself lounging in a verdant field that you suddenly realize is the mean kind of green—poison ivy, poison oak, or sumac—do not panic. Disinfect as quickly as possible with rubbing alcohol and paper towels, followed by soap and water.

❾ Battle of the Bugs

Summer bugs are a picnic plague. Bring an arsenal of citronella votives and bug spray. To keep unwelcome sweet-tea swimmers at bay, try this easy trick for transforming a Mason jar: Remove the lid and set it aside. Take a square of decorative paper, punch a hole in it, lay it over the lip of your jar, replace the ring, and poke a straw through the hole. Drink elsewhere, bugs.

❿ Extras! Extras!

In anticipation of tomorrow night's disaster, when you'll be staring at your empty refrigerator longing for picnic fare, invest in a stack of takeout boxes, and end the evening by trading leftovers.

Lawn Games Scoring Guide

Everyone loves to play outdoor games, but no one can ever remember how to keep score. Mollify the melee by bookmarking this page for ready reference at the picnic.

BADMINTON

Setup: Stake the net and determine boundaries for the court.

How to play: Flip a coin to determine who serves first. Score 1 point by acing a serve or winning a rally. Play three games of 21 points to determine the winner of the match. (The winning team serves first in the next game.)

Tricky rule: If the score is 20–20, the first team to gain a 2-point lead wins the game.

CAPTURE THE FLAG

Setup: Divide the park into two territories. Designate a clear boundary, two jails, and a starting place.

How to play: Give each team three minutes to plant its flag. (Flags must be placed two hundred steps from the starting place, in plain view.) Shout "Go!" From this point, play lasts one hour. The aim of the game is to capture the opposing team's flag through subterfuge and strategy. Win the game by either capturing the flag and returning it to your territory, or capturing the most prisoners.

Tricky rule: You must stay 50 feet away from your team's flag, unless an enemy crosses into that territory. To capture an enemy, tag him, shout "Caught!" three times, and throw him in jail. Prisoners can be rescued one at a time if tagged by a teammate. If a prisoner is captured while holding the flag, drop the flag where the prisoner was caught and continue to play.

PÉTANQUE AND BOCCE

Setup: Find a court, or improvise on a flat patch of grass. Stand next to your opponent and throw a target ball 18 to 30 feet away.

How to play: Split into two teams. Flip a coin to see who goes first. For bocce, each team of two to four players receives four balls. For pétanque, each player in a two-person game receives three boules, or balls. The aim of the game is to land the most boules near the target, either by tossing accurately or by savagely knocking the opponents' boules off course. Once all the boules have been played, the team with the boule closest to the target wins. To score the game, award one point to the winning team for every boule that's inside the losing team's boules.

Tricky rule: What's the difference between pétanque and bocce? Pétanque players must stand still and toss the boule palm down, while bocce players can take a few steps and bowl the boule palm up. Also, the boules look different. That's pretty much it.

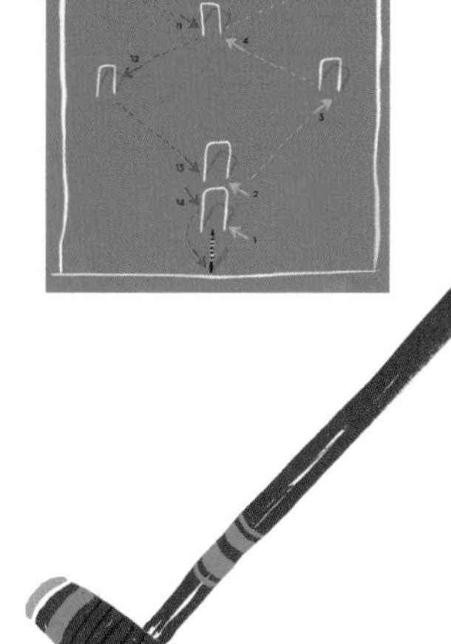

CROQUET

Setup: Emulate the setup at right.

How to play: The aim of the game is to hit a ball through the wickets, in order. If a player hits a ball through a wicket, she is awarded an additional turn. If a player knocks an opponent's ball aside, she earns an additional two turns. Win by finishing the course first.

Tricky rule: Curiously, the order of play is color-coded. Blue plays first, then red, black, yellow, green, and orange. If teams are playing, blue, black, and green form one team; red, yellow, and orange form the other team.

CORNHOLE

Setup: Position opposing cornhole boards 27 feet apart.

How to play: Split into two teams of two players. Stand facing your partner and, alternating with your opponent, throw four beanbags, one at a time, toward the board. Score 1 point for landing on the board and 3 points for making a basket. Score each round by subtracting the losing team's score from the winning team's score. The first team to reach 21 wins.

Tricky rule: The winner of each round throws first in the next round. If the score is tied, alternate sides.

What's in Your Basket?

The Definitive Packing List

Stock your basket with the following necessities so you'll be ready to picnic at a moment's notice.

ESSENTIALS

- [ ] Picnic blanket
- [ ] Cutlery
- [ ] Napkins
- [ ] Plates
- [ ] Glasses or Mason jars
- [ ] Serving spoons
- [ ] Serving forks
- [ ] Wine opener
- [ ] Small cutting board
- [ ] Opinel folding knife
- [ ] Containers for leftovers
- [ ] Four bags for cleanup (trash, recycling, compost, dirty dishes)
- [ ] Paper towels
- [ ] Bug spray
- [ ] Matches & candles
- [ ] Moist towelettes
- [ ] The food!

EXTRAS

- [ ] Portable record player
- [ ] Common condiments kit (see page 20)
- [ ] Wineglass stakes
- [ ] Scissors
- [ ] Pitcher
- [ ] Gallon of water
- [ ] Salad tongs
- [ ] Card or folding table
- [ ] Beach umbrellas
- [ ] First-aid kit
- [ ] Tablecloth (108 inches)
- [ ] Whisk and mixing bowl
- [ ] Lawn games
- [ ] Chef's knife
- [ ] Portable cocktail bar
- [ ] Zester

STRIKE ONE
MATCHES
d
S

CHAPTER 2

Bites

Bites are the embodiment of picnic politesse—easy to eat, they encourage conversation; plentiful, they have a way of stretching an afternoon into the evening; convenient, they're finger-friendly; fresh, they celebrate the season. We love a party where everyone pitches in, but at times a picnic spread can be so plentiful that it's overwhelming. These petite treats are always a welcome addition to the mix. A smattering of small bites can create a complete, tapas-style meal or serve as starters to accompany larger dishes.

The Essential Deviled Egg

The best deviled egg recipe is one that easily shifts to your culinary whims. This recipe is delicious on its own, garnished with a dash of cayenne or a pinch of chopped chives, but turn to page 36 for a dozen divine new identities.

MAKES 1 DOZEN

6 large eggs, hard-cooked and peeled

½ cup D.I.Y. Mayonnaise (recipe follows) or store-bought mayonnaise

1 teaspoon Dijon mustard

½ teaspoon Champagne vinegar

Pinch of fine sea salt

IN THE BASKET:

- ☐ **Egg whites in plastic container**
- ☐ **Bag of filling (inside bag of ice) + scissors**
- ☐ **Garnish**
- ☐ **Serving plate (bonus points for a bona fide deviled egg platter)**

1. Halve each egg lengthwise, pop out the yolks, and press them through a potato ricer into a small bowl. Rinse the egg whites and pat dry.
2. Whisk together the mayonnaise, mustard, vinegar, and salt in a medium bowl. Add the egg yolks and whisk the filling until smooth.
3. Spoon the filling into a 1-quart resealable plastic bag, or a pastry bag fitted with a ½-inch fluted tip, and chill it until the picnic, or for up to 48 hours. (Cover the tip in plastic wrap before screwing the plastic ring into place.) Transport the filling to the picnic in a cooler or 1-gallon resealable plastic bag filled with ice.
4. At the picnic, snip a corner of the plastic bag, or unseal your pastry bag, and squeeze about 1 tablespoon of filling into each egg white. Serve to wild applause, real or imaginary.

Easy Egg Salad

It's just a tiny leap from deviled eggs to egg salad. If it's egg salad you're after, simply whisk together the mayonnaise, mustard, and vinegar; chop the hard-cooked eggs; and fold them together. If using any of the optional additions from the Deviled Dozen, add them to the mayonnaise mixture before you fold in the chopped eggs. Serves 4.

D.I.Y. Mayonnaise

Homemade mayonnaise trumps store-bought any day, and it's straightforward to make. Try this once and next time you'll be whipping up a batch in minutes.

MAKES 1⅓ CUPS

2 large egg yolks (preferably fresh eggs from a farmers' market)
2 teaspoons cider vinegar
1 teaspoon Dijon mustard
½ teaspoon fine sea salt
¾ cup vegetable oil
¼ cup mild extra-virgin olive oil
2 teaspoons fresh lemon juice
Pinch of freshly ground pepper

TINY TIP: If the mayonnaise separates after some of the oil is added, the emulsion has broken. To fix a broken mayonnaise, whisk together 1 egg yolk and 1 teaspoon water in a clean bowl. While whisking constantly, slowly drizzle in the broken mayonnaise. When it has all emulsified, continue adding the remaining oil and proceed as directed in the recipe.

Put the egg yolks, vinegar, mustard, and salt in a food processor and pulse until combined. Scrape the sides of the bowl with a rubber spatula as needed. With the motor running, begin adding the vegetable oil in a slow stream, then the olive oil, until it emulsifies and thickens. Scrape the sides of the bowl again. When the emulsion has formed, begin adding the oil in a faster stream until it is all incorporated. If at any point after the emulsion forms the mayonnaise becomes too thick, add about ½ teaspoon of the lemon juice to loosen it, and continue. To finish, pulse in the lemon juice and pepper, then taste and adjust the seasoning. Store the mayonnaise for up to 1 week in an airtight container in the refrigerator.

Aioli Variation

With a chef's knife, mince 1 garlic clove, then sprinkle it with salt and mash to a paste using the edge of the knife blade. Add the garlic paste to the food processor at the beginning along with the egg mixture, then proceed to add the oil as directed in the recipe. Thin the emulsion with a splash of water for a saucy consistency.

The Deviled Dozen

1. Angels on Horseradish

Filling: 2 tablespoons grated fresh horseradish; ½ teaspoon white pepper; pinch of salt
Garnish: Radish wings

2. Old Bay

Filling: ¼ cup minced celery; 1 tablespoon minced red onion; 1½ teaspoons Old Bay seasoning; 1 teaspoon grated lemon zest
Garnish: Bay shrimp

5. Chorizo A-Go-Go

Filling: 1 teaspoon smoked Spanish paprika; 1 small garlic clove, minced
Garnish: Matchstick of chorizo

6. Olive You, Deviled Egg

Filling: 2 tablespoons store-bought olive tapenade
Garnish: Half a pitted Niçoise olive

9. Pesto Chango

Filling: 2 tablespoons pesto
Garnish: Tiny fresh basil leaves

10. B.L.T.

Filling: ¼ cup minced cooked bacon
Garnish: ½ cherry tomato; ½-inch strip bacon; butter lettuce

Give the Essential Deviled Egg (page 34) a twist by adding a few simple ingredients to the master filling recipe, and topping with garnishes.

3. Green Goodness

Filling: 1 tablespoon minced fresh tarragon; 1 tablespoon minced green onions
Garnish: Tarragon sprig; thinly sliced green onions

4. Gremolata

Filling: ½ teaspoon minced garlic; 1 tablespoon grated lemon zest; 2 tablespoons minced fresh flat-leaf parsley
Garnish: Strip of lemon zest

7. Comrade Yolk

Eggs: See page 60 for pickling instructions
Filling: 2 tablespoons finely chopped fresh dill; 1 tablespoon sour cream
Garnish: ¼ teaspoon caviar

8. Smoked Salmon and Dill

Filling: 2 tablespoons minced fresh dill; 1 teaspoon minced capers
Garnish: Dill sprig; capers

11. Curry in a Hurry

Filling: 1 teaspoon curry powder
Garnish: Mango slice; turmeric

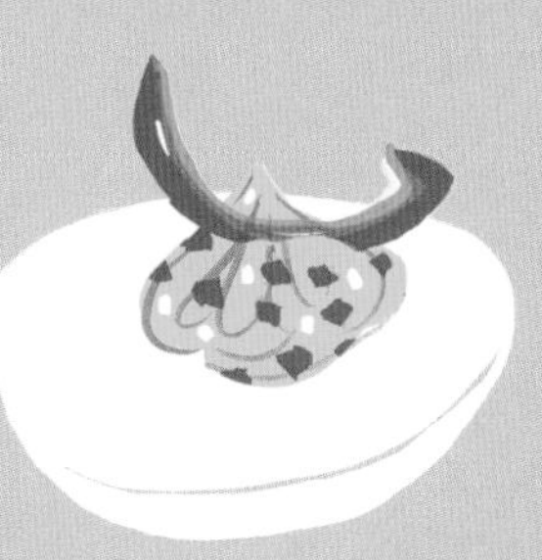

12. Southern Comfort

Filling: Two 2-ounce jars diced pimentos, drained; 1 tablespoon grated white onion; ½ cup finely grated extra-sharp Cheddar
Garnish: Red pepper strip

A Deviled Egg Primer

What elevates these snacks from standard to sublime? Technique, technique, technique. Follow these tips and tricks to create a deviled egg worthy of competing with Grandma's.

A Good Egg

A lump-free filling starts with properly hard-cooked eggs. Using a slotted spoon, gently lower room-temperature eggs into boiling water. Cook for 13 minutes, adjusting the heat to maintain a gentle boil. Remove the eggs and immediately plunge them into an ice bath to cool and prevent an unsightly gray halo from surrounding the perfectly cooked (pale yellow and crumbly) yolks.

Crack 'Em Up

Remove the shell without damaging the egg by tapping the egg and then rolling it on the counter, cracking the shell into zillions of pieces. Peel the egg under water, starting at the bubble on the bottom. Slice each egg in half lengthwise with a sharp knife.

Rice, Rice Baby

Whether you mash them with a fork, toss them into a food processor, press them through a fine-mesh sieve à la James Beard, or squish them through a food mill à la Julia Child, breaking up the yolks into consistent, teeny pieces leads to a smooth filling. We suggest you use a potato ricer. One quick squeeze and you're done. That said, if you're deviling dozens and dozens, a food processor works best.

It's the Little Things

To preserve the filling's creamy consistency, use a Microplane to grate additional ingredients like onion, garlic, vegetables, cheese, and citrus zest.

Picnic Theater

Give them dinner and a show. Assembling your eggs on-site entertains onlookers and allows you to sidestep the stigma of arriving at the soirée bearing an already congealing creation. Fresh is best.

Transport

But if you insist on filling your eggs at home, ferry your little devils to the park in style. Nestle them in a tiffin, which has plenty of headspace, and put ice in the tier below the eggs. Or invest in an egg keeper, the cupcake carrier of the picnic-obsessed.

Classy Crudités

During picnic season, when produce is at its prime, crudités can be a grace note for any picnic spread. Elevate this easy-to-assemble dish using only a knife, a jar, and the punchy tzatziki-inspired Dilly Dip (page 40).

My Own Private Crudités

Using 4-ounce jelly jars, make small vegetable arrangements and serve them individually. You'll be lauded by lovers of tiny food and germophobes alike.

The Tricolore

Select mouthwatering, exciting produce: romanesco broccoli (steamed for 3 minutes, then shocked in an ice bath), breakfast radishes, and sweet snap peas. Spoon into a clear jar (which will also function as your serving dish) in enticing layers of contrasting colors.

The Pinwheel

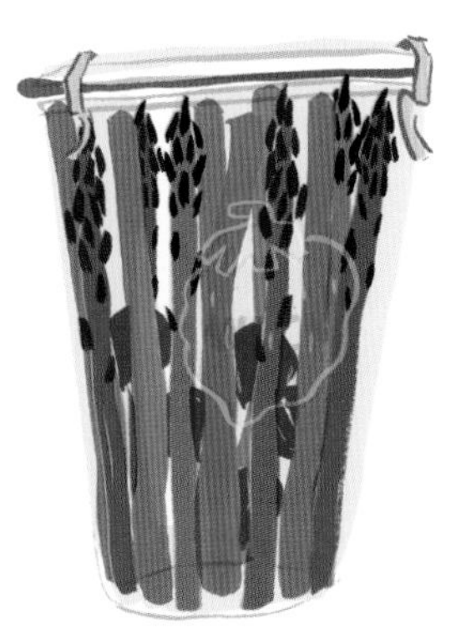

Arranging crudités in artful circles creates this veritable vegetable diorama. Trim eight (or so) carrot sticks and eight (or so) asparagus spears to the height of a wide-mouthed jar. Lay the jar on the table and line the inside of half the jar with alternating carrots and asparagus. Now fill the jar half-full with radishes to weight the standing vegetables. Rotate the jar to line the other half with alternating carrots and asparagus, shifting the radishes to hold the vegetables in place. Set the jar right side up on the table, continue the pinwheel with another circle of tall crudités (cucumbers, celery, and wax beans work well), and then fill the middle with the remaining radishes, or another bright vegetable, like romanesco broccoli or purple cauliflower.

Four Snappy Snacks

Even the most unassuming pantry staples can be transformed into a royal picnic dish. Here's a handful of nibbles that will never fail you.

1. Prosciutto-Wrapped Grissini

MAKES 12

12 grissini (thin, crisp Italian breadsticks)

6 paper-thin slices prosciutto, at room temperature

Gently cut or tear each slice of prosciutto in half lengthwise, and carefully spiral each section around the top half of a grissini. If a few of them snap, don't fret—just eat the evidence and proceed. Smooth the ends until secure, and serve on a platter or standing upright in a glass jar weighted with dried beans.

2. Dilly Dip with Pita Chips

MAKES 1¾ CUPS

DIP

½ English cucumber

1 cup Greek-style yogurt

½ cup sour cream

3 tablespoons minced fresh dill

1 garlic clove, minced

2 teaspoons fresh lemon juice

½ teaspoon fine sea salt

½ teaspoon freshly ground pepper

PITA CHIPS

1 bag pita bread

¼ cup extra-virgin olive oil

Za'atar (page 100)

Fine sea salt

For the dip: Grate the cucumber on the medium holes of a box grater. Put the grated cucumber in a kitchen towel and squeeze to remove the excess juice. Place all the ingredients in a 1-pint glass jar and shake vigorously until mixed well.

For the pita chips: Preheat the oven to 350°F. Using a pizza wheel or sharp knife, cut the pita bread into 10 wedges; spread them in a single layer on a rimmed baking sheet. Brush each side with oil, sprinkle them with za'atar and salt, and bake until crisp and golden brown, 12 to 15 minutes. Cool, then store for up to 2 weeks in an airtight container.

3. Pecorino Popcorn with Tarragon

SERVES 4 TO 6

3 tablespoons extra-virgin olive oil
1 tablespoon dried tarragon
2 tablespoons vegetable oil
½ cup popcorn kernels
½ teaspoon fine sea salt
1 cup finely grated Pecorino

Heat the olive oil and tarragon in a small pot over low heat until fragrant. Meanwhile, heat the vegetable oil and popcorn over high heat in a large pot with a tight-fitting lid. When the first kernel pops, shake the pot off the heat, then return it to the heat. Shake every 10 seconds or so until the popping slows, then remove the pot from heat for good. Pour the warm oil over the popcorn, sprinkle with salt, replace the lid, and shake the pot vigorously. Working in layers, pour half of the popcorn into a metal bowl, sprinkle half of the Pecorino over it, and stir to mix. Repeat and adjust the salt if necessary.

4. Cannellini Greenie Crostini

MAKES 36 CROSTINI

CROSTINI

1 baguette
½ cup extra-virgin olive oil
Kosher or sea salt

BEANS AND GREENS

One 15-ounce can cannellini beans, drained and rinsed
½ cup pitted green olives, preferably picholine
½ cup grated Parmigiano-Reggiano
3 tablespoons extra-virgin olive oil
¼ cup chopped fresh flat-leaf parsley, plus tiny sprigs for garnish
1 teaspoon grated lemon zest
2 tablespoons fresh lemon juice
¼ teaspoon freshly ground pepper

For the crostini: Preheat the oven to 350°F. Thinly slice the baguette, and spread the rounds in a single layer on two rimmed baking sheets. Brush each side with oil and sprinkle with salt. Bake for 20 to 25 minutes, until crisp and golden brown, rotating the baking sheets halfway through. Cool, then store for up to 2 weeks in an airtight container.

For the beans and greens: Combine the beans, olives, cheese, oil, parsley, lemon zest and juice, and pepper in a food processor and pulse to a coarse purée. At the picnic, spread a thick layer on each of 36 crostini. Garnish each with a tiny sprig of parsley.

Cheese Expertise

So many cheeses, so little space on your board, what's a picnicker to do? We turned to one of the world's top cheese sages, Steve Jones—the owner of Portland's destination cheese shop, Cheese Bar, and the winner of the Cheesemonger Invitational—for the how-to on assembling a lineup of winning wedges.

1. Let the "Holy Trinity" be your guide. Opt for one cow, one sheep, and one goat milk cheese for three distinct flavors.
2. As far as quantity is concerned, a quarter pound each of three cheeses is a good rule of thumb for a group of six. Or estimate a total of two ounces of cheese per person.
3. Looks matter. Vary your cheese by color: alabaster Brie, pale gold Comté, ash-layered Morbier, blue-veined Stilton, and titian Gouda always impress.
4. Mix and match textures, too. Alternate a craggy, extra-aged Manchego, semifirm Garrotxa, and a gooey round of Saint-Marcellin.
5. Accent with fun accoutrements. Nuts, fresh and dried fruit, chutney, honey, olives, cornichons, whole-grain mustard, salumi, and artisan crackers all make delicious playmates for your cheeses, or simply tear off hunks of fresh baguette.

6. No fancy serveware required. All you really need is a suitable surface (a nice wooden cutting board will do just fine) and a butter knife, if you don't have a cheese service set.

7. Don't sweat it. Unless it's the hottest day of the summer and you happen to have a cooler handy, don't worry about chilling your cheese en route. "The nice thing about cheese is that it wants about an hour to warm up anyhow, so if you have an hour between your fridge and eating, it's perfect; you're just doing the cheese a favor," Jones says.

8. Be informative. People like the skinny on what they're eating, so prepare a mini curds class. Introduce each cheese by type and origin, or check our Picnic Provisions (page 185) for cute cheese signs. To make your own signs, cut up an index card, summon your best calligraphy, and stick them into a few halved wine corks split partway through. Voilà, you've got easy cheese labels.

EXTRA CREDIT: THE TROPHY CHEESE TREASURE HUNT

If the group you're serving is particularly cheese savvy, you may want to hunt down what Jones refers to as a "trophy cheese," like Vermont-based Jasper Hill's Harbison—a spruce bark-wrapped bloomy rind that he suggests you score in an X, peel back the flaps, and serve with shaved ham and walnut bread.

Meet Your Meat: Building Beautiful Charcuterie Boards

Salami, salumi; loma, lardo; coppa, capicola—building the perfect charcuterie board can be as confusing as learning the Italian language, but it's really a cinch to lay out a beautiful board in minutes. We went directly to the source to collect tips and tricks—meat maven Michelle Cairo of Olympic Provisions just happens to be in our picnic circle, and she always puts together a glorious charcuterie board.

❶ Choose a *Charcutier*

Select an artisan charcuterie shop or a deli that does good business so you're sure to buy cured meat that isn't dried out from sitting in a cold case for too long.

❷ Choose a Salami

Opt for two different kinds, geared toward your theme if you have one—for example, two distinct kinds of chorizo if you're having a Spanish picnic, two Italian salami if your picnic is Italian-themed. Forgo ordering in poundage and ask the butcher or deli staff for three slices of each salami per person; so for a party of six, you'll leave with eighteen slices of soppressata and eighteen slices of genoa. If the meat board is one of the picnic's main dish attractions, double that.

❸ Choose Complementary Cured Meats

Why stop at salami? Include everyone's favorite melon hugger, prosciutto, or other common deli-case residents such as coppa, capicola, lomo, and lardo. Again, plan on three slices of each per person.

❹ Choose a Forcemeat

This category includes pâtés, terrines, rillettes, and pork, chicken, or duck liver mousse, to name a few. Plan on 4 ounces per six people. After positioning the spread on the board, drizzle it lightly with olive oil and sprinkle it with cracked black pepper.

❺ Choose a Pickle

Your Quickle Pickle (page 59) skills are sorely needed here; the rich, fatty quality of charcuterie begs for the acidity provided by pickled vegetables. Fennel, beets, shallots, and giardiniera are all excellent choices.

❻ Choose Accoutrements

A generous dollop or small dish of whole-grain mustard and one thinly sliced artisan baguette or batch of Crostini (page 41) later, and you're ready to unveil your meaty masterpiece.

❼ Choose a Presentation

First, you'll need a board; just a simple wooden cutting board is best. Section it six ways to accommodate the salami, cured meats, forcemeat, pickled vegetables, mustard, and sliced baguette or crostini. You can assemble your board at the picnic site for a theatrical touch, or you can shop for ingredients ahead of time, then lay them out before you leave, wrap it tightly in plastic wrap for transport, and tote it to the picnic intact. If it's a hot day, ferry the board in a cooler or bag over ice to prevent the charcuterie from sweating in summer heat.

Oysters on the Half Shell

One day at the park back when we were picnic novices (yes, there was such a time), we observed a stylish group one oak tree over pull a sack of fresh oysters from their basket, deftly shuck them, and start slurping. This seemed to be the height of picnic sophistication, and we were transfixed. Now you can be that envied urbanite, with the flick of an oyster knife and these easy accoutrements. If you fear the oyster knife, bring a dish to your fishmonger and ask her to shuck the oysters for you.

SERVES 12

2 teaspoons minced shallots
2 tablespoons Champagne vinegar
Pinch of freshly ground pepper
2 dozen oysters
¼ cup cocktail sauce
2 tablespoons freshly grated horseradish
1 lemon, cut into wedges

1. Mix the shallots, Champagne vinegar, and pepper in a 4-ounce jelly jar to make Champagne mignonette.

2. Arrange the oysters on a platter mounded with crushed ice and wrap tightly for transport. At the picnic, shuck the oysters and serve them with the mignonette, cocktail sauce, horseradish, and lemon wedges.

IN THE BASKET:

- ☐ **Oyster knife (if planning to shuck on-site)**
- ☐ **Mignonette**
- ☐ **Cocktail sauce**
- ☐ **Prepared horseradish**
- ☐ **Lemon wedges**

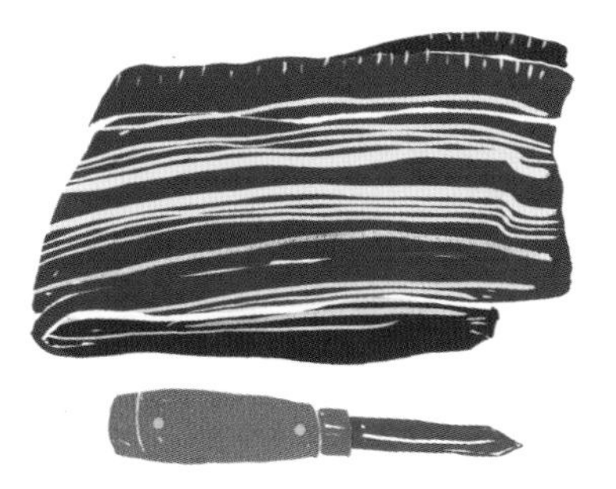

1. Gather your shucking equipage—a kitchen towel, an oyster knife (see Picnic Provisions, page 185), and your wits.

2. Lay the oyster on the towel, hinge toward you. Fold the towel over the oyster, pinning it down securely.

How to Shuck an Oyster sans Bodily Harm

It was a brave picnicker who first ate an oyster, but an even braver one who shucked it. Shuck off your shucking fears and slurp sooner in four easy steps.

3. Slowly push the knife point through the hinge and toward the bottom of the oyster, then twist until the shell pops open. Run the knife around the edge of the upper shell, then under the meat, until the oyster is free.

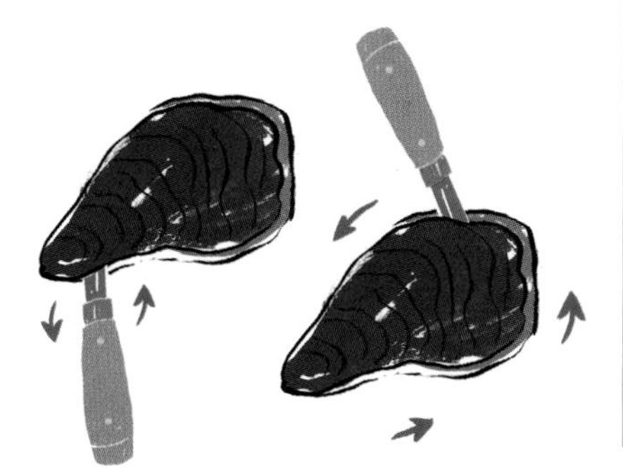

4. Procure some bubbly to go with your bivalves and enjoy.

Savory Rosemary Pecan Sandies
with Marmalade

This cousin of the classic English biscuit is gorgeous, buttery, and even more scrumptious when topped with a dollop of punchy marmalade. And since there's no shame in having a standby dish, consider keeping a batch at the ready. The dough will keep for two days in the refrigerator or up to one month in the freezer. When the picnic arises, just slice, bake, grab a jar of marmalade from the pantry, and go.

MAKES 16 TO 20

1 cup roasted unsalted pecans, plus 16 to 20 pecan halves

1 cup all-purpose flour, plus more for kneading

8 tablespoons (1 stick) cold unsalted butter, cubed

1 tablespoon light brown sugar

2 teaspoons minced fresh rosemary

1 teaspoon fine sea salt

2 to 3 tablespoons ice-cold water

Jar of orange marmalade

IN THE BASKET:

- ☐ **Marmalade + tiny spoon**

1. Pulse the cup of pecans in a food processor until very finely chopped. Add the flour, butter, sugar, rosemary, and salt and process to the texture of coarse meal. With the motor running, drizzle in 2 tablespoons water and continue processing until the dough comes together like wet sand; add up to another tablespoon of water if needed.

2. Dump the dough onto a lightly floured countertop and briefly knead it together. Transfer to the center of a sheet of parchment paper (or plastic wrap). Using the parchment paper, pat and roll the dough into a cylinder about 2 inches in diameter. Roll it up tightly in the parchment and twist the ends closed. Refrigerate the cylinder of dough until firm, at least 1 hour and up to 2 days before baking.

3. Position racks in the upper and lower thirds of the oven and preheat it to 350°F.

4. Unwrap the cylinder of dough and cut it into ⅓-inch-thick rounds. Place the rounds at least 1 inch apart on two baking sheets, and press a pecan half into the center of each. Bake until the sandies are crisp and light golden brown on the bottoms and just beginning to color at the edges, rotating the pans halfway through, 16 to 20 minutes. Cool, then pack in a covered container between layers of parchment paper to transport to the picnic. Serve marmalade alongside, with a small spoon for spreading.

Ripe Figs
with Feta and Honey

Anyone would be lucky to picnic with Mona Johnson; she works for the Portland Farmers' Market, which means she always brings relentlessly seasonal dishes to the blanket. These feta-topped figs are the perfect example, and they take mere minutes to assemble.

MAKES 12

- 6 ripe green or black figs
- Twelve 1-inch square feta cubes
- Honey for drizzling
- 12 mint leaves, thinly sliced

Slice the figs in half lengthwise. Put one cube of feta atop each fig half, place all on a platter, and wrap with plastic. At the picnic, drizzle them with honey and sprinkle mint over the top. Never have you done so little work for so much adulation.

IN THE BASKET:

- ☐ **Honey + honey dipper**
- ☐ **Mint**

Menu: Flamenco Feast

These tasty tapas will dance their way into your heart (and your stomach).

Melon Gazpacho

This quintessentially summery soup takes on a captivating coral hue in this bright, blender-friendly fix. Pour it straight into jars with tight-fitting lids, garnish, chill, and go.

SERVES 4 TO 6

1 large cucumber, peeled, halved lengthwise, and seeded

One 3-pound cantaloupe, quartered, seeded, scooped from the peel, and coarsely chopped

1 roasted red bell pepper, peeled, seeded, and coarsely chopped

⅓ cup coarsely chopped red onion

2 tablespoons fresh lime juice, plus more as needed

Fine sea salt

⅓ cup Greek-style yogurt

2 tablespoons finely chopped fresh mint

IN THE BASKET:

- ☐ Spoons

1. Coarsely chop half of the cucumber and put it in a blender with the cantaloupe, roasted pepper, onion, lime juice, and ½ teaspoon salt. Blend until finely puréed, about 2 minutes. Taste and adjust the seasoning with additional lime juice or salt as needed. Divide the gazpacho among individual 8-ounce jars.

2. Finely dice the remaining cucumber. Mix it together in a small bowl with the yogurt, mint, and a pinch of salt. Spoon a dollop of the garnish into each jar of gazpacho. Cover and refrigerate until cold, or for up to 8 hours before the picnic.

Provençal Puffs

To make these ahead of time, just prepare the batter as directed, store it in a gallon-size resealable plastic bag, and freeze for later. Come party day, thaw, snip the corner of the bag, and puff away.

MAKES 24 PUFFS

- 8 tablespoons (1 stick) unsalted butter, cubed, plus more for greasing the sheets
- ½ cup milk, plus more for brushing
- 1 teaspoon fine sea salt
- 1 cup all-purpose flour
- 4 large eggs
- 10 oil-packed anchovy fillets, drained and very finely minced, or 2 teaspoons anchovy paste
- ½ cup grated Parmigiano-Reggiano
- ¼ teaspoon freshly ground pepper

IN THE BASKET:

- ☐ **Serving basket + pretty kitchen towel**

1. Preheat the oven to 400°F. Lightly grease two rimmed baking sheets.
2. Bring the butter, milk, and salt to a boil in a medium saucepan over medium-high heat. Remove the pan from the heat and stir in the flour using a wooden spoon. Return the pan to the heat and beat the dough vigorously with the spoon until it's smooth and glossy and pulls away from the sides of the pan, about 1 minute. Set aside to cool for 2 to 3 minutes.
3. Beat in the eggs one at a time, making sure that each is completely incorporated before adding the next, stirring vigorously. Add the anchovies, about two-thirds of the cheese, and the pepper along with the last egg. Stir well to combine.
4. Transfer the dough to a pastry bag with a ½-inch round tip. Squeeze out dollops of dough, about 1 inch in diameter, onto the prepared baking sheets, spacing them at least 1 inch apart. Brush lightly with milk and sprinkle with the remaining cheese. Bake until puffy and golden, about 20 minutes. Cool, then package the puffs in a container for transport.

Smoked Salmon Tartare
on Cucumber Rounds

Few bites elicit more oohs and aahs than these gorgeous smoked-salmon-topped cucumber slices, and it's your secret that they're one of the easiest recipes ever.

MAKES 18

- 1 teaspoon fresh lemon juice
- ½ teaspoon grated lemon zest
- 1 teaspoon toasted sesame oil
- 1 tablespoon finely sliced fresh chives
- 1 teaspoon grated fresh ginger
- 1 teaspoon black sesame seeds, plus more for garnish
- 4 ounces smoked salmon, finely chopped
- 1 English cucumber sliced in ¼-inch rounds

IN THE BASKET:

- ☐ **Serving platter, if desired**

1. In a medium bowl, whisk together the lemon juice and zest, sesame oil, chives, ginger, and sesame seeds. Stir in the chopped salmon.
2. Place a teaspoon of salmon mixture in the center of each cucumber round, then garnish with a pinch of black sesame seeds for extra decorative oomph. Arrange them in a single layer in a large rectangular baking dish and cover tightly with plastic wrap for transport.

Menu: Oh My, Omakase

For maximum impact, serve this Asian-inspired picnic under a blossoming cherry tree. Don't forget chopsticks.

Smoked Salmon Tartare on Cucumber Rounds 54

Vietnamese Noodle Bowls with Shrimp and Vegetables 110

Japanese jarred salad (with mizuna, orange, green onion, and snap peas) 66

Japanese Potato Salad 92

Chocolate-Dipped Green Tea Shortbread 134

Shiso Pretty Iced Tea 167

Chicken Liver Mousse
with Lillet Gelée

Fragrant, floral, and *French*, the aperitif Lillet is one of our favorite picnic sips. We like it so much we put it in our chicken liver mousse in lieu of the traditional brandy or Cognac for a light, warm-weather variation. This creamy mousse can be scooped right from the jar and spread on crackers or toasted brioche, and be sure to bring along a jar of Fennel Trifecta (page 60) to garnish.

MAKES 2 CUPS

Mousse

8 ounces chicken livers
6 tablespoons unsalted butter, softened
1 cup chopped yellow onion
½ cup sliced peeled tart apple
1 teaspoon fresh thyme leaves
3 tablespoons Lillet
2 tablespoons heavy cream
½ teaspoon fine sea salt
⅛ teaspoon freshly ground pepper

Lillet Gelée

⅓ cup plus 1 tablespoon Lillet
1 teaspoon sugar
¼ teaspoon unflavored powdered gelatin

IN THE BASKET:

- ☐ **Serving knife**
- ☐ **Fennel Trifecta + tiny fork**
- ☐ **Crackers, Crostini (page 41), or toasted brioche rounds**

1. To make the mousse: Cut the chicken livers into 1-inch pieces, removing sinew or greenish spots, if there are any. (We appreciate your dedication.)

2. Melt 2 tablespoons of the butter over medium-low heat in a hot sauté pan. Add the onion, apple, and thyme and sauté until the onion is translucent and just beginning to brown and the apple slices are tender, about 5 minutes. Add the livers and sauté until they are firm but pink inside, 3 to 5 minutes. Pour in the Lillet and increase the heat to medium-high. Simmer until the liquid is almost dry, about 2 minutes. Remove the pan from the heat and let cool.

3. When the chicken liver mixture is still warm but not piping hot, scrape it into a blender. Add the remaining 4 tablespoons butter, the cream, salt, and pepper. Blend on high speed to a creamy, exceptionally smooth purée, about 2 minutes. Pour the purée into two 8-ounce, widemouthed glass canning jars, leaving a ½-inch headspace. Cover and refrigerate until the mousse is completely chilled and thickened, 1 to 2 hours.

4. To make the gelée: Bring ⅓ cup of the Lillet and the sugar to a boil in a small saucepan, stirring until the sugar dissolves. Continue boiling about 1 minute to cook off most of the alcohol.

5. Meanwhile, put the remaining 1 tablespoon of Lillet in a small bowl and sprinkle the gelatin over it. Let stand until absorbed, about 1 minute.

6. Pour the boiling Lillet mixture into the bowl of softened gelatin and stir to dissolve. Cool until the gelée is at or slightly above room temperature, then pour it over the top of each jar of mousse, dividing it evenly. Cool until set, 45 minutes to 1 hour. Cover the jars and refrigerate for up to 3 days.

Shocking-Pink Beet Hummus

Ho-hum hummus gets a makeover when roasted beets are blended into the mix. Serve with pita bread, pita chips, or Classy Crudités (page 39) for dipping.

MAKES ABOUT 2 CUPS

1 medium red beet, top trimmed, scrubbed

1¾ cups cooked chickpeas, or one 15-ounce can, drained and rinsed

3 tablespoons tahini

Juice of 1 large lemon

2 tablespoons water

1 large garlic clove, smashed

1 teaspoon fine sea salt

Extra-virgin olive oil

Chopped fresh flat-leaf parsley

IN THE BASKET:

- ☐ **Pita chips or pita bread**
- ☐ **Crudités**
- ☐ **Squeeze bottle of olive oil**
- ☐ **Parsley**

1. Preheat the oven to 375°F. Wrap the beet in aluminum foil and place it in the oven in a small baking dish. Roast until very tender when pierced with a fork, about 1 hour. Unwrap the foil and set the beet aside to cool. Once cool enough to handle, peel and coarsely chop.

2. Put the beets, chickpeas, tahini, lemon juice, water, garlic, and salt in a food processor and purée until smooth, 2 to 3 minutes. Taste and adjust the seasoning.

3. Transfer the hummus to a container for transport, cover, and refrigerate until the picnic, or for up to 1 week. For extra pizzazz, just before serving, drizzle the hummus with oil and sprinkle with parsley.

Quickle Pickles

These speedy pickles keep in the refrigerator for up to a month, so you'll always be prepared should a picnic pop up. Use this basic brine as a guide and experiment with flavor combinations by substituting different herbs, spices, vinegars, and vegetables (see page 60).

MAKES ABOUT 1 QUART

- 12 ounces pickling cucumbers, such as Kirby
- 8 dill sprigs
- 4 large garlic cloves, thinly sliced

Brine

- 1 tablespoon fennel seeds
- 1¼ cups white wine vinegar
- 1 cup water
- 2 tablespoons honey
- 1½ tablespoons fine sea salt

1. Wash and dry the cucumbers well. Trim any stems and quarter the cucumbers lengthwise into spears. Pack the spears into a widemouthed 1-quart glass jar along with the dill sprigs and garlic.
2. To make the brine: Heat a medium saucepan over medium heat. Add the fennel seeds and swirl the pan constantly, until fragrant and lightly toasted, about 30 seconds. (Be careful not to burn the seeds or they will become bitter.) Off the heat, pour in the vinegar, water, honey, and salt. Bring the brine to a strong boil over high heat, stirring until the honey and salt are dissolved. Pour the boiling brine into the jar to completely cover the vegetables. (Reserve any leftover brine, and return it to a boil to pickle something else.)
3. Set the jar aside and allow the brine to slowly come to room temperature. When completely cooled, after at least 2 hours and up to 4 hours, cover the jar and refrigerate the pickles until the picnic, or for up to 1 month.

You Can Pickle That

Don't stop at cucumbers when it comes to quick pickling; just about any vegetable you bring home from the farmers' market or pull out of your garden can be thrown into a jar, covered with brine (see page 59), and pickled to your heart's content. Here are seven of our favorite variations.

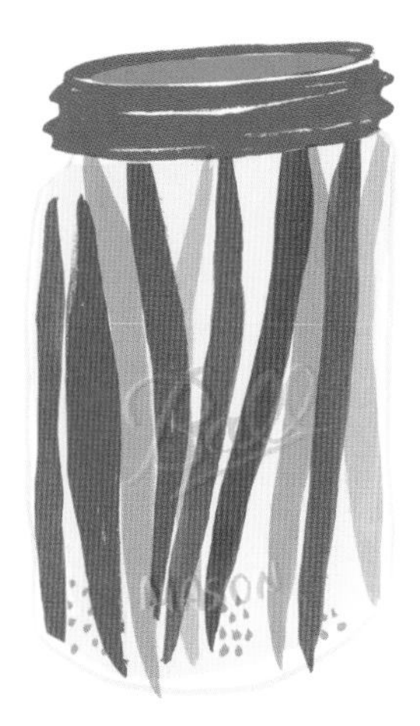

Rainbow Carrots

Substitute 12 ounces large peeled rainbow carrots cut into spears for the cucumbers.

Comrade Yolk

To make the stunners for Comrade Yolk Deviled Eggs (page 37), substitute 6 hard-cooked eggs and 1 small red beet, roasted, peeled, and sliced into rounds, for the cucumber. Omit the garlic. Shake the jar periodically to ensure an even color.

Fennel Trifecta

Substitute 1 large (12- to 14-ounce) fennel bulb, cut into wedges, for the cucumbers and fennel fronds for the dill.

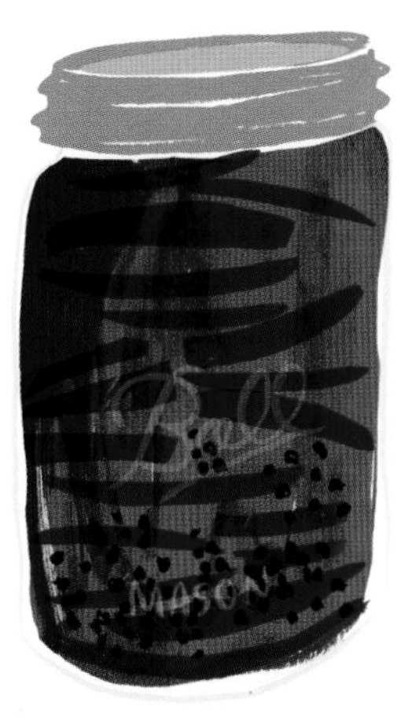

We Got the Beets

Substitute 12 ounces red or golden beets, roasted, peeled, and sliced into rounds, for the cucumber. Omit the garlic and add ¼ teaspoon black peppercorns.

Dilly Beans

Substitute 12 ounces trimmed green beans for the cucumbers.

Giardiniera

Substitute ¾ cup each of diced red pepper, sliced celery, sliced carrots, and cauliflower florets and 3 seeded and quartered fresh pepperoncini peppers for the cucumbers. Substitute fresh oregano for the dill and add ½ teaspoon red pepper flakes and ½ teaspoon black peppercorns.

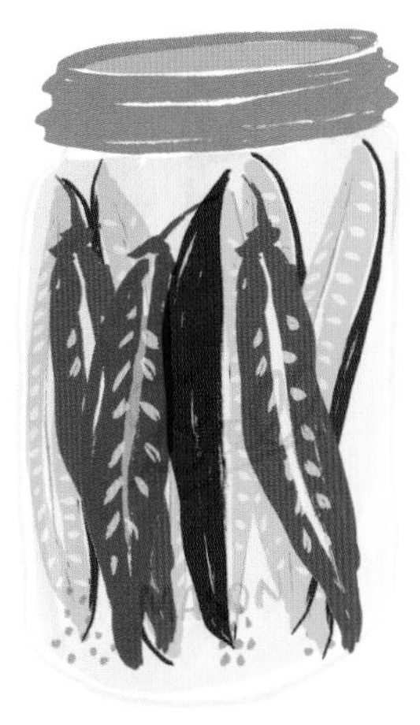

Spicy Pickles

Halve or quarter 1 or 2 small, hot red or green chiles and put them in the jar with any of the vegetables in these variations before pouring in the brine.

Tortilla Española
with Fava Beans and Romesco

Spain's national dish is a four-season pleaser, but adding fava beans spells spring. Make this dish within a few hours of departing for your picnic to prevent the green favas from dyeing the eggs a grayish hue, and keep it at room temperature until serving. If you need to make this ahead, skip the favas for a classic variation.

SERVES 8 TO 10

Romesco Sauce

1 dried ancho (pasilla) chile

⅓ cup diced tomatoes

2 tablespoons sherry vinegar

¼ cup roasted hazelnuts

2 garlic cloves

1 roasted red bell pepper, stemmed, peeled, and seeded

2 tablespoons dried bread crumbs

1 large egg yolk

1½ teaspoons fine sea salt

3 tablespoons extra-virgin olive oil

Tortilla

1 pound fava beans in the pod

¼ cup extra-virgin olive oil

12 ounces small Yukon Gold potatoes, peeled and thinly sliced into rounds

1 pound spring onions, green tops and roots trimmed, white bulbs halved and thinly sliced

1½ teaspoons fine sea salt

Freshly ground pepper

8 large eggs

IN THE BASKET:

- ☐ **Serving knife**
- ☐ **Jar of romesco + spoon**

1. To make the romesco sauce: Slit the dried chile lengthwise and discard the stem and seeds. Tear or chop it into little pieces and place them in a small bowl with the tomatoes and vinegar to rehydrate for about 30 minutes. Put the hazelnuts and garlic in a food processor and pulse to finely mince. Add the tomato mixture, the roasted pepper, bread crumbs, egg yolk, and salt and process to a coarse purée. With the processor running, slowly drizzle in the olive oil through the feed tube. Taste and adjust the seasoning with salt or vinegar, if needed. Transfer the romesco to a small jar with a lid.

2. To make the tortilla: Fill a medium saucepan with water and bring it to a boil over high heat. Prepare a large bowl of ice water. Remove the fava beans from their pods. Boil the beans for 30 seconds, then drain and plunge them into the ice bath to stop the cooking. When they're cool, tear open the skins and pinch the beans into a small bowl, discarding the skins.

3. Heat the oil in a 9- to 10-inch cast-iron skillet or ovenproof nonstick sauté pan over medium-high heat. Add the potatoes, onions, 1 teaspoon of the salt,

and pepper to taste. Reduce the heat to medium and cook, stirring occasionally, until the onions are very soft and translucent and the potatoes are tender when pierced with a fork, about 15 minutes.

4. Position an oven rack about 4 inches from the top heating element and preheat the broiler.

5. Beat the eggs together with the remaining ½ teaspoon of salt in a large bowl. Stir the fava beans into the potato-onion mixture, spread the vegetables evenly in the pan, and pour in the eggs. The eggs should just barely cover the vegetables. Reduce the heat to medium-low and cook until the eggs are almost set but still liquid on top, 10 to 15 minutes. Transfer the pan to the oven and broil until the top is set and golden brown, about 3 minutes. Cool the tortilla to warm or room temperature.

6. Transport the tortilla to the picnic in the pan, wrapped with aluminum foil, or transfer it to a platter. To unmold, run a dull knife or spatula around the edges of the pan. Place a platter on top of the pan and invert the tortilla. Slice it into wedges and serve with the romesco sauce on the side.

CHAPTER 3

Salads

Lettuce still dewy from the garden, tomatoes warm from the vine, sweet corn ready to be husked, fava beans shelled on the porch—there's really no finer expression of summer than its harvest, and what better way to showcase it than in a salad. Whether you're keen on greens, grains, tubers, or taproots, these beautiful, bountiful dishes bring the best out of your garden or local farm stand. Here you'll find enough ideas for chopping, slicing, and tossing produce to last all summer long.

A Jumble of Jarred Salads

Crack the code to a satisfyingly crisp salad in a jar in six simple steps.

1. Pack the jar like a grocery bag, with hardy ingredients at the bottom and delicate ingredients on the top. Any jar will do, but 500-ml Weck jars are a particularly perfect portion for these salads.
2. Mix 2 tablespoons dressing with a crunchy vegetable in the bottom layer of the salad.
3. Stack wet or briny ingredients (cucumbers, olives) in the second layer.
4. Sprinkle seeds, nuts, fruit, or cheese in the next layer.
5. Pile tender herbs or greens on the top.
6. Once you arrive at the picnic, invert the salad a few times to toss. Open and enjoy!

Japanese

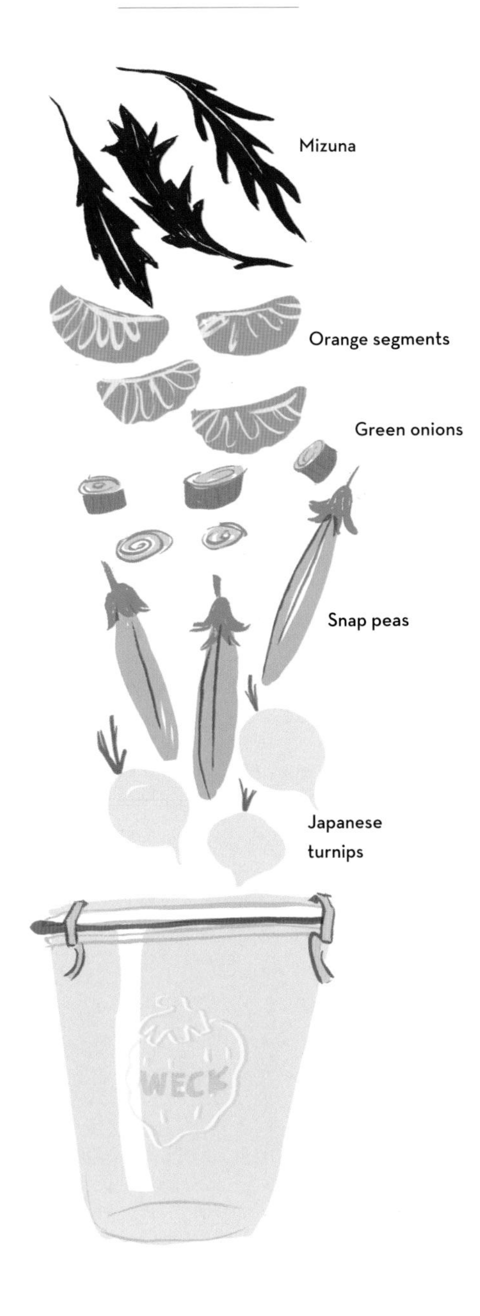

Italian
Arugula
Salami
Provolone
Fennel
Chickpeas
WECK
Greek
Sun Gold
tomatoes
Feta
Olives
Cucumber
Red onion
WECK

A Trio of Fruit Salads

While strawberries, oranges, bananas, grapes, and melon make a plenty-nice mix, fruit salad can be so much more than the five familiars. Here are three handsome new takes. Each serves 4 to 6 picnickers.

Cherries, Pistachios, and Mint

If you are fond of wine and dread having to pit cherries, you'll love this fun trick—drink a bottle of wine, then place cherries, one at a time, atop its neck, and use a chopstick to send the pit plummeting into the empty bottle. Then proceed with making this supremely simple but spectacular mint-kissed salad. Toss together 1 pound of stemmed, pitted, and halved fresh Bing or Rainier cherries; ½ cup shelled roasted salted pistachios; and ¼ cup thinly sliced fresh mint leaves.

Peaches, Burrata, and Basil

Could there possibly be a better combination than sweet summer peaches, fragrant basil, and a luscious lump of burrata? We think not. Place one 8-ounce ball of burrata in the center of a wide, shallow serving dish, arrange four large pitted and quartered peaches around the outside, and sprinkle them with ¼ cup of thinly sliced fresh basil leaves, fine sea salt, and freshly ground pepper. Drizzle it all with extra-virgin olive oil. (For extra flavor, brush the peach wedges with oil and grill them until lightly charred.)

Watermelon, Feta, and Black Olives

For added artistic impact, use different varieties of watermelon to create a red, orange, and yellow melon masterpiece dotted with bright crumbles of feta and striking black olives. Prepare the salad right in a jar to create an easily transported, ready-made centerpiece. Layer 1-inch watermelon squares in a 1-quart glass jar with 3 ounces crumbled feta, 3 ounces pitted Kalamata olives, and 1 teaspoon chopped fresh summer savory or mint.

Ooh-La-La Niçoise

Arrange this stunning salad in colorful stripes on a platter, but transport it to the picnic with the help of a tiffin (see page 19), which separates the goods into individual layers for a smooth transition from your kitchen to the park.

SERVES 4 TO 6

- 1 pound red or yellow baby potatoes
- Fine sea salt
- 8 ounces green beans, preferably haricots verts, trimmed
- 8 ounces multicolored cherry tomatoes, halved
- 1 large cucumber, quartered lengthwise and cut into bite-size pieces
- 1 bunch radishes, trimmed and cut into small wedges
- 4 eggs, hard-cooked (see page 38), peeled, and quartered
- ½ cup Niçoise olives, drained
- 12 fresh basil leaves
- Two 4-ounce tins albacore tuna packed in olive oil
- Shallot Shake-Up Vinaigrette (recipe follows)
- Aioli (page 35)

IN THE BASKET:

- ☐ **Serving spoons for dressing + aioli**
- ☐ **Small fork for tuna**
- ☐ **Salad server**

1. Put the potatoes in a medium saucepan, add water to cover by at least 2 inches, and season with salt. Bring to a boil over high heat, then reduce the heat and simmer until the potatoes are tender when pierced with a fork, about 15 minutes. Drain in a colander and set aside to dry and cool, then cut in half.

2. Meanwhile, fill a small saucepan with water, season it generously with salt, and bring it to a boil over high heat. Add the beans and cook until crisp-tender, about 3 minutes. Drain, rinse under cold water, then dry the beans in a kitchen towel.

3. Pack the potatoes, beans, tomatoes, cucumber, radishes, eggs, olives, and basil in separate containers or resealable plastic bags. At the picnic site, arrange the components of the salad side by side on a large platter, keeping them separate so that picnickers can assemble their own blend of ingredients. Tear the basil leaves into pieces and scatter them over the top of the salad. Open the tins of tuna and nestle them on the platter. Serve the vinaigrette and aioli on the side.

Shallot Shake-Up Vinaigrette

MAKES ABOUT 1 CUP

- 1 large shallot, minced
- 2 garlic cloves, minced
- 2/3 cup extra-virgin olive oil
- 1/4 cup fresh lemon juice
- 1 tablespoon Dijon mustard
- 1 teaspoon fine sea salt
- 1/2 teaspoon freshly ground pepper

Put all the ingredients in an 8-ounce Mason jar with a tight-fitting lid and shake vigorously to emulsify. Taste and adjust the seasoning. Refrigerate for up to 1 week.

Menu: An Herbivore's Hootenanny

For a meat-free good time, call on this brightly hued, vegetable- and fruit-forward spread.

Roasted Wax Beans
with Colatura, Olives, and Oregano

A mix of summer beans gets a hit of umami thanks to a spoonful of colatura. Made by layering anchovies and salt in wooden barrels and then collecting the salty anchovy essence as it drips down, colatura is the Italian version of fish sauce. Like its Southeast Asian cousin, a little bit goes a long way. You can find it online or at your favorite specialty market, but if it proves tricky to track down, substitute the good old Thai or Vietnamese version, which can be found in most grocery stores.

SERVES 8 TO 12

2 pounds green and yellow wax beans, ends trimmed

2½ tablespoons extra-virgin olive oil

½ teaspoon fine sea salt

1 tablespoon colatura or Thai or Vietnamese fish sauce

1 tablespoon fresh lemon juice

1 tablespoon chopped fresh oregano

½ teaspoon freshly ground pepper

¾ cup black olives, such as Kalamata, Gaeta, or Cerignola, smashed, pitted, and coarsely chopped

IN THE BASKET:

- ☐ **Salad server**

1. Put a large rimmed baking sheet in the oven and preheat the oven to 450°F.

2. Toss the beans in a large bowl with the oil and salt. When the oven is hot, remove the baking sheet and spread the beans on it evenly. Roast, stirring just once halfway through, until lightly charred and crisp-tender, 10 to 12 minutes.

3. Cool the beans to room temperature, then put them back in the large bowl and toss with the colatura, lemon juice, oregano, and pepper. Taste and adjust the seasoning. Transfer the beans to a bowl for transport and top with the olives. Cover and take to the picnic or refrigerate up to 1 day.

Kale Panzanella
with Burnt Lemon Caesar Dressing

To complement kale's robust flavor, upgrade classic Caesar with smoky, charred lemons. You'll crave their complexity and admire the dramatic touch they add to your salad bowl.

SERVES 4 TO 6

- 2 lemons, halved crosswise
- 2 large egg yolks
- 2 tablespoons freshly grated Parmigiano-Reggiano, plus more for garnish
- 2 oil-packed anchovy fillets, drained
- 2 garlic cloves
- ½ teaspoon sugar
- Fine sea salt
- ¼ teaspoon freshly ground pepper
- ⅓ cup plus 2 tablespoons extra-virgin olive oil
- 4 cups 2-inch cubes artisan bread
- 1 teaspoon minced fresh rosemary
- 2 bunches kale, washed and dried well, coarsely chopped

IN THE BASKET:

- ☐ **Salad server**
- ☐ **Croutons**
- ☐ **Extra dressing**

1. Heat a stovetop grill pan or cast-iron skillet over high heat. When it's smoking hot, place the lemons in the pan, cut sides down, and sear until nicely charred, about 2 minutes. Squeeze the juice from one of the lemon halves to get about 2 tablespoons; reserve the remaining lemons for garnish.

2. Whirl the lemon juice, egg yolks, cheese, anchovies, garlic, sugar, ½ teaspoon salt, and the pepper in a blender until smooth. With the motor running, drizzle in ⅓ cup of the oil through the hole in the lid in a slow stream until the dressing emulsifies and thickens. Stop and scrape the sides of the blender as needed. Transfer the dressing to a small container, cover, and refrigerate for up to 3 days.

3. Position an oven rack about 4 inches from the top heating element and preheat the broiler. Toss the bread chunks with the remaining 2 tablespoons oil and a pinch of salt and spread them out in an even layer on a rimmed baking sheet. Broil the bread, stirring occasionally, until evenly charred and crisp on the outside but still

a little soft within, 3 to 5 minutes. While still hot, sprinkle the croutons with the rosemary and toss to coat. Cool completely, then transfer the croutons to a resealable plastic bag.

4. Just before leaving for the picnic, toss the kale with just enough of the dressing to lightly coat. Taste and adjust the seasoning. Transfer the salad to a serving bowl. Use a vegetable peeler to shave large flakes of Parmigiano-Reggiano over the top and place the charred lemons around the edges of the bowl. Cover to transport to the picnic. Toss the croutons into the salad at the picnic site; before serving, squeeze in a little of the charred lemons' juice, and add more dressing, if needed.

Salads on a Stick

We've deconstructed six classic salads, from Caprese to Cobb, and rearranged them on toothpicks (4-inch bamboo knot skewers work beautifully) to craft these one-bite wonders.

EACH RECIPE MAKES 12

Waldorf

Mix 1 teaspoon lemon zest into 4 ounces room-temperature chèvre. Cut 2 celery ribs into 1-inch lengths and chop 2 tablespoons of walnuts. Cut half a green apple into ⅛-inch-thick slices and soak them in lemon juice to prevent browning. Press 1 teaspoon of the chèvre mixture into each piece of celery and dip into walnuts. Spear an apple slice and a Concord grape, then anchor with celery.

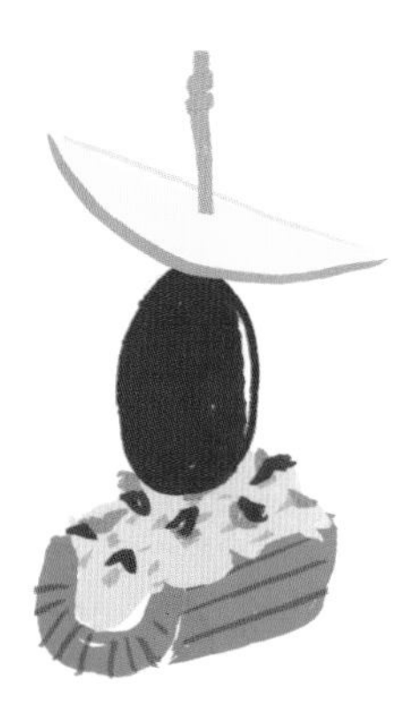

Caprese

Slice 6 cherry tomatoes in half and remove seeds and pulp. Roll a mini mozzarella ball (ciliegine) in salt and pepper and nestle it inside a tomato cup. Trim 12-inch wooden skewers to varied lengths. Insert the wooden skewers so the mozzarella is on top, and skewer a basil leaf atop each to garnish. Transport the skewers flat in a plastic container and arrange in a bouquet at the picnic, using a tall, heavy jar as a vase.

Cobb

Ask the butcher for a ½-inch-thick slice of ham or turkey. Cut it into ¾-inch squares. Skewer each square with half of a hard-cooked quail egg, a cherry tomato, a ½-inch segment of cooked bacon, and a cube of blue cheese.

Melonpoleon

Cut a pineapple, watermelon, and several kiwis into ½-inch-thick slices. Cut out rounds from each fruit slice using a 1½-inch biscuit cutter, twisting as you push down to create clean layers. Stack the fruit, top with a mint leaf and a raspberry, and skewer.

Potato

Boil 6 baby potatoes (the smallest you can find) until fork-tender, about 7 minutes. Slice in half crosswise, place in a bowl, and toss the hot potatoes with ¼ cup Shallot Shake-Up Vinaigrette (page 71). Cover the bowl with a kitchen towel for 5 minutes. Skewer, flat side down, with a wedge of hard-cooked egg and a cornichon.

Greek

Slice three ½-inch-thick rounds from the widest part of an English cucumber and quarter them into four equal sections. Skewer a cherry tomato, a ½-inch square of feta, a pitted Kalamata olive, and a sliver of red onion, then anchor with the cucumber wedge.

Menu: Mezzepalooza

Transform your picnic into a moveable souk.

Greek Salad on a Stick 77

Shocking-Pink Beet Hummus 58

Watermelon, Feta, and Black Olives 69

Za'atar Lamb Meatball Pitas 100

Brick-Roasted Chicken with Zucchini and Apricot Couscous 122

Pistachio Pomegranate Soda Floats 128

Triple Mint Tea 167

Picnic Attire

Strictly speaking, picnics do not require a dress code, but you'll have the best possible time if you heed the following tips on outfitting.

1. Not Feelin' Those Heels

Nothing upends an Apricot Almond Franny (page 152) faster than a stiletto stuck in the grass. Opt for wedges, sandals, or bare feet.

2. Hey Shorty

If you find yourself spending more time worrying about inadvertently displaying your derriere than listening to the riveting conversation, save that teeny-tiny dress/skirt/romper for date night.

3. Sunnies Day

Sunglasses are practically required at a picnic. But it's all too easy to step on stray sunnies adrift on the blanket. Remember to bring your sunglasses case, or see 99 Ways (and Counting) to Use a Mason Jar (page 24) for an alternative.

4. Brimming with Joy

Slather on sunscreen before departing for your picnic, and be sure to bring a hat to shield your face. Not only is it better for your skin, but it's also your best bet against peculiar tan lines.

5. Hold on to That Handbag

Yes, you should always look on the sunny side of life, but that doesn't mean there aren't shady characters in the park. Prevent pickpocketing by keeping your adorable bag on your adorable body.

6. Baby, It's Cold (-ish) Outside

Even if the thermometer insists it's a balmy 90°F, when the sun goes down, you'll feel chilly. Bring a cardigan, wrap, or throw blanket to prevent the party from ending early. And since you were clever enough to remember yours, tote an extra for your friend who forgot hers.

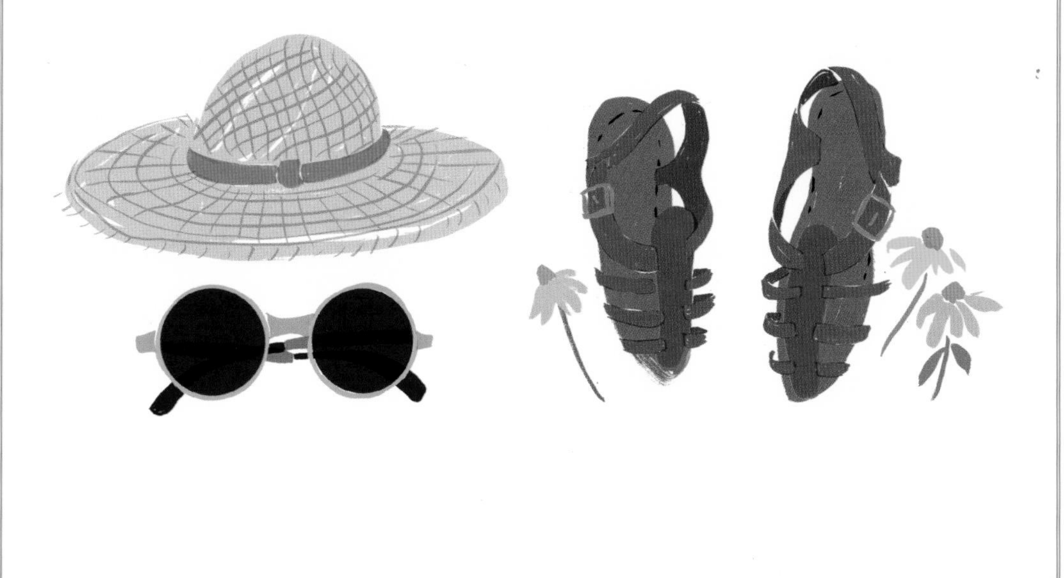

Asparagus and Fava Beans
with Poppy Seed Vinaigrette

Your blanket buddies will swoon at this exquisite combination of bright green favas, asparagus spears, and chives set atop a bed of delicate mâche. If mâche proves to be elusive, substitute baby spinach leaves, watercress, or purslane.

SERVES 4 TO 6

- Fine sea salt
- 1 pound fava beans in the pod
- 1 pound asparagus, trimmed and cut on a sharp angle into 2-inch spears
- 3 ounces ricotta salata, cut into ¼-inch cubes (about ½ cup)
- ⅓ cup fresh chives snipped into 1-inch segments
- 3 tablespoons extra-virgin olive oil
- 2 tablespoons cider vinegar
- 1 tablespoon honey
- 2 teaspoons Dijon mustard
- 1 teaspoon poppy seeds
- ⅛ teaspoon freshly ground pepper
- 6 cups loosely packed mâche or baby spinach leaves

IN THE BASKET:

- ☐ Serving spoons

1. Fill a medium saucepan with water, season it generously with salt, and bring it to a boil over high heat. Prepare a large bowl of ice water.

2. Remove the fava beans from their pods. Boil the beans for 30 seconds, then transfer with a slotted spoon to the bowl of ice water. When they're cool, tear open the skins and pinch the beans out into a large bowl, discarding the skins.

3. Return the water to a boil, add the asparagus, and cook until just tender, 3 to 4 minutes. Drain and transfer to the ice water, then drain again when completely cooled. Toss the asparagus, ricotta salata, and chives with the fava beans.

4. Whisk together the oil, vinegar, honey, mustard, poppy seeds, ½ teaspoon salt, and the pepper in a small bowl. Stir the dressing into the asparagus mixture. Taste and adjust the seasoning. (The salad can be refrigerated for up to 4 hours at this point.)

5. Just before leaving for the picnic, pile the mâche into the bottom of a wide, shallow serving bowl. Mound the asparagus salad over the top and cover tightly for transport.

Farro Tricolore
with Balsamic-Fig Dressing

Sweet figs, crunchy walnuts, and creamy mozzarella make for a tremendously satisfying whole-grain salad, which features emmer farro, an heirloom variety of wheat berries.

SERVES 4 TO 6

¾ cup emmer farro
Fine sea salt
2 sprigs fresh thyme plus ½ teaspoon chopped fresh thyme
½ small head radicchio, cored and cut crosswise into ½-inch-thick strips
4 dried Mission figs, finely chopped
1 garlic clove, minced
3 tablespoons extra-virgin olive oil
2 tablespoons balsamic vinegar
1 teaspoon honey
¼ teaspoon freshly ground pepper
¾ cup chopped walnuts, toasted
5 cups baby arugula leaves
6 ounces ciliegine (cherry-size) mozzarella balls, halved

IN THE BASKET:

☐ **Serving spoons**

1. Put the farro in a medium saucepan with 3 cups water, ½ teaspoon salt, and the 2 thyme sprigs. Bring to a simmer over high heat. Reduce the heat to maintain a low simmer and cook, partially covered, until the farro is tender but still quite chewy, 45 minutes to 1 hour. Drain, rinse under cold water until cool, then drain again. Discard the thyme.

2. Meanwhile, soak the radicchio in a large bowl of ice-cold water for 45 minutes to 1 hour to remove some of the bitterness and make it crisp. Drain and dry it well.

3. Put the figs and garlic in a small bowl and pour in ¼ cup steaming-hot tap water to barely cover. Set aside until cooled, about 15 minutes.

4. Whisk together the oil, vinegar, honey, 1 teaspoon salt, the chopped thyme, and pepper in a medium bowl. Add the fig mixture and stir to combine.

5. Combine the farro and the dressing in a large bowl. Add the radicchio and walnuts and mix it all together. Toss in the arugula and mozzarella just before the picnic.

Candy-Striped Beet, Fennel, and Apple Coleslaw

Toss your preconceived notions of slaw out the window. This gorgeous version exchanges cabbage and carrots for fragrant fennel, crisp apple slices, and thinly sliced Chioggia beets.

SERVES 4 TO 6

- 2 tablespoons cider vinegar
- 2 teaspoons honey
- 2 teaspoons Dijon mustard
- ½ teaspoon celery seeds, toasted
- ½ teaspoon fine sea salt
- ¼ cup extra-virgin olive oil
- 2 medium Chioggia beets (or golden beets, if Chiogga beets are not available)
- 1 large fennel bulb with fronds attached
- 1 large tart apple
- 1 tablespoon sunflower seeds

IN THE BASKET:

- ☐ Serving spoons

1. Combine the vinegar, honey, mustard, celery seeds, and salt in a large bowl and whisk it all together. Slowly drizzle in the oil while whisking constantly.

2. Peel the beets and slice them as thinly as possible using a mandoline. Put the beets in the bowl with the dressing. Trim and discard the green stalks from the fennel bulbs, reserving up to ⅓ cup of the fronds; coarsely chop the fronds and set them aside. Trim the root end and cut the fennel bulb in half lengthwise. Cut out the triangular core from each half. Thinly slice the fennel into strips.

3. Cut the apple in half and trim away the core. Thinly slice the apples and add them to the bowl with the beets and fennel. Toss it all together until evenly mixed and coated well in the dressing. Marinate the slaw for at least 30 minutes at room temperature, or up to 8 hours in the refrigerator, before the picnic. Toss the fronds and sunflower seeds into the slaw just before serving.

Farmers' Market Macaroni Salad

Toss seasonal vegetables from the farmers' market into this throwback-salad-turned-modern-marvel. (It couldn't be further from the deli-case variety.) This mac salad hits all the right notes.

SERVES 4 TO 6

- Fine sea salt
- 2 cups elbow macaroni
- 1½ cups ½-inch florets broccoli or romanesco
- ½ cup finely diced carrots
- ½ cup finely diced red onion
- 8 ounces cherry tomatoes, halved (about 1½ cups)
- ½ cup finely diced yellow bell pepper

Dressing

- ¾ cup D.I.Y. Mayonnaise (page 35) or store-bought mayonnaise
- ½ cup buttermilk
- 3 tablespoons chopped fresh flat-leaf parsley
- 2 tablespoons ketchup
- 1 tablespoon cider vinegar
- 2 teaspoons Dijon mustard
- 1 teaspoon sugar
- 1 teaspoon fine sea salt
- ½ teaspoon freshly ground pepper

IN THE BASKET:

- ☐ Serving spoons

1. Bring a large pot of water to a boil, season it generously with salt, and cook the macaroni until al dente according to the package directions. About 1 minute before the macaroni is done, add the broccoli and carrots to the pot and cook until just tender. Drain in a colander and rinse under cold water to stop the cooking. Drain well and transfer to a large bowl.

2. Meanwhile, soak the onion in a small bowl of cold water for at least 10 minutes to remove its harsh bite. Drain and add the onion to the bowl with the pasta mixture, along with the tomatoes and bell pepper, and stir it all together.

3. To make the dressing: Whisk together the mayonnaise, buttermilk, parsley, ketchup, vinegar, mustard, sugar, salt, and pepper in a large bowl. Add the pasta mixture and stir well to coat. Cover and refrigerate until chilled and the flavors meld, at least 1 hour and up to 2 days. Transfer to a serving bowl and cover tightly for transport to the picnic.

Rainbow Carrots
with Smoky Paprika Vinaigrette

Part of the fun of preparing this vibrant salad stems from searching for just the right mix of heirloom carrots, in a spectrum spanning from deep purple to bright yellow to ivory. (Good old orange works, too.) We prefer sweet (dulce) smoked Spanish paprika, or pimentón de la Vera, in this recipe, rather than the hot (picante) variety; look for it at specialty grocery stores.

SERVES 4 TO 6

¼ cup extra-virgin olive oil
1½ tablespoons sherry vinegar
1 teaspoon honey
½ teaspoon fine sea salt
¼ teaspoon sweet smoked Spanish paprika
1 pound rainbow carrots
1½ cups cooked chickpeas or one 15-ounce can, drained and rinsed
½ cup dried plums (prunes), chopped
¼ cup chopped fresh mint

1. Whisk together the oil, vinegar, honey, salt, and paprika in a large bowl until emulsified; set aside.
2. Shave carrots into ribbons (see sidebar on the opposite page).
3. Add the carrots, chickpeas, dried plums, and mint to the bowl with the vinaigrette, and toss well so that everything is coated nicely and thoroughly mixed together. Taste and adjust the seasoning. Transfer the salad to a portable container and refrigerate until the picnic, or up to 8 hours.

IN THE BASKET:
- ☐ Salad server

The Carrot Trap

The best way to achieve ribbons of carrots that meld flawlessly with the smoky sherry vinaigrette is by shaving the carrots. Yes, you read that correctly.

1. Peel and discard the tough outer layer from the carrots and trim the tops.
2. Pin the tip of the carrot to a cutting board using a fork, and shave it into long ribbons with a vegetable peeler until you reach the core.
3. Flip the carrot and continue shaving until, again, you reach the core.
4. Pile the gorgeous tangle of carrot ribbons into your salad bowl, and toss the cores to your dog, who's giving you side eye. He'll thank you.

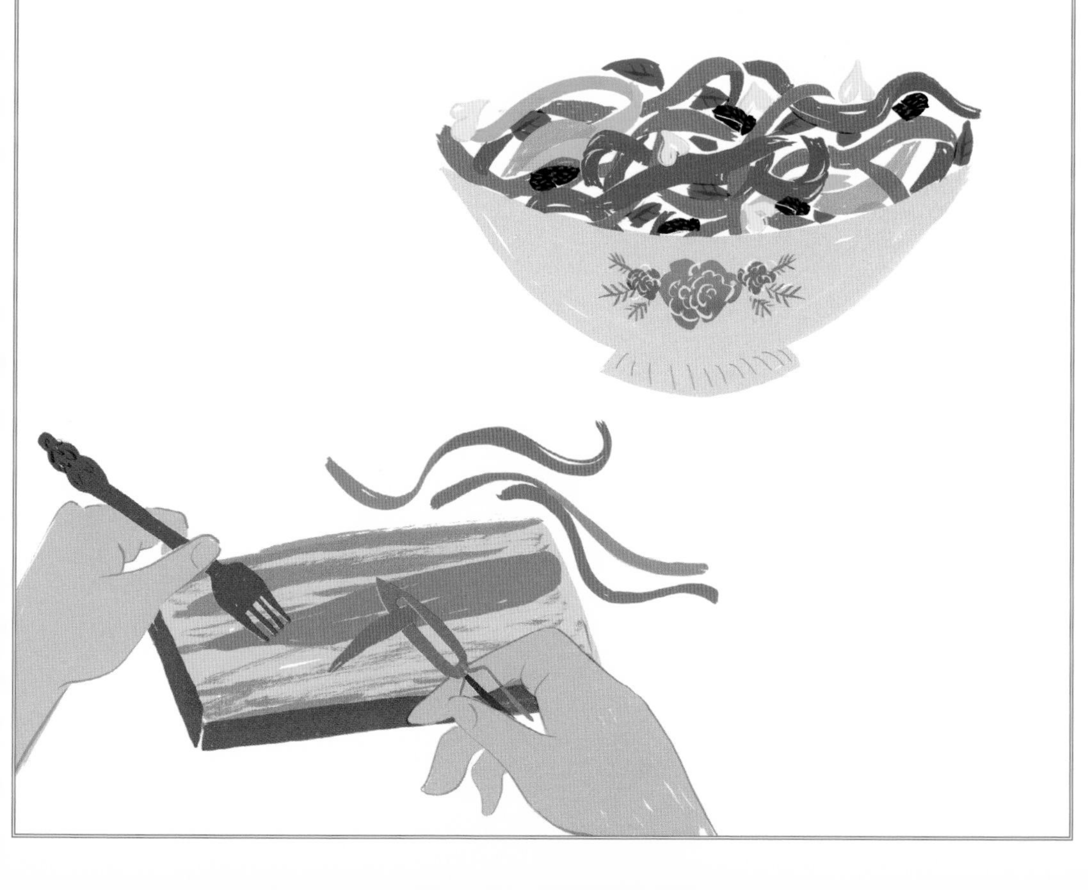

Cabbage, Pineapple, and Spiced Pepita Slaw

Crisp slivers of cabbage mingle with sweet corn, radishes, pineapple, warm spices, and fresh herbs to create a gorgeous tangle of eye candy.

SERVES 4 TO 6

4 cups very finely shredded green cabbage

1 bunch radishes, thinly sliced

1 cup diced fresh pineapple

⅔ cup cooked sweet corn

3 green onions, white and green parts, thinly sliced diagonally

⅓ cup chopped fresh cilantro

3 tablespoons plus 1 teaspoon extra-virgin olive oil

2 tablespoons fresh lime juice

½ teaspoon fine sea salt

¼ teaspoon freshly ground pepper

3 tablespoons Honey Spiced Pepitas (recipe follows)

1. Submerge the cabbage in a large bowl of cold water for about 30 minutes to eliminate the bitterness and make it extra crunchy.
2. Drain the cabbage and dry it well in a salad spinner or kitchen towel. Combine the cabbage, radishes, pineapple, corn, onions, and cilantro in a large bowl. Drizzle with the olive oil and the lime juice, sprinkle with the salt and the pepper, and toss to combine well. Transfer the slaw to a portable container for the picnic and garnish with the pumpkin seeds. For the best texture, serve within 1 hour.

IN THE BASKET:

- ☐ Serving spoons

Honey Spiced Pepitas

MAKES 1/2 CUP

- 2 teaspoons extra-virgin olive oil
- 1/2 cup raw pumpkin seeds (pepitas)
- 1/2 teaspoon ground cumin
- 1/4 teaspoon ground cinnamon
- 1/4 teaspoon fine sea salt
- Pinch of cayenne
- 1 teaspoon honey

Heat the oil over medium-low heat in a 10-inch sauté pan, preferably nonstick. Add the pumpkin seeds and sauté until lightly toasted, about 2 minutes. Add the cumin, cinnamon, salt, and cayenne and sauté until the pumpkin seeds are evenly toasted, about 2 minutes more. Stir in the honey and continue cooking just until it clings to the seeds, about 30 seconds more. Transfer the pumpkin seeds to a large plate and spread them in a single layer. Cool to room temperature.

Tomato, Peach, and Corn Salad
with Crumbled Feta

Every summer without fail, our friend Lila Martin pops up at a picnic with this summer trio: a mixture of ripe red tomatoes, juicy peaches, and sweet corn. Because of the produce's delicate nature, toss this together just before heading out to your picnic.

SERVES 4 TO 6

Fine sea salt

2 ears yellow sweet corn, shucked

½ cup thinly sliced red onion

1 pound ripe peaches, halved, pitted, and cut into 1-inch chunks

1 pound multicolored heirloom tomatoes, cored and cut into 1-inch chunks

3 tablespoons extra-virgin olive oil

2 teaspoons Banyuls or Moscatel vinegar

1 tablespoon chopped fresh sweet summer herb, such as summer savory, tarragon, basil, or mint

¼ teaspoon freshly ground pepper

2 ounces sheep milk feta cheese

IN THE BASKET:

- ☐ **Serving spoons**

1. Fill a medium pot with water, season it generously with salt, and bring it to a boil over high heat. Add the corn and cook until bright yellow and just tender, about 5 minutes. Drain the corn and cool it in a bowl of ice water, then pat dry. Stand the ears on end and cut off the kernels with a sharp knife; discard the cobs. Put the corn in a large bowl.

2. Meanwhile, soak the onion in a small bowl of cold water for at least 10 minutes to remove its harsh bite. Drain and add the onion to the bowl with the corn, along with the peaches and tomatoes. Drizzle with the oil and vinegar and sprinkle with the herb, ½ teaspoon salt, and the pepper. Toss it all together, then taste and adjust the seasoning. Transfer the salad to a serving bowl and crumble the feta over the top. Cover tightly for transport to the picnic.

An Alfresco Food Safety Seminar

Here's a (well-washed) handful of food safety tips to ensure that the only bugs present at your picnic are the kind that can be seen and swatted.

Wash It, Wash It Good • At a picnic, washing facilities can be limited, so be sure to pack hand sanitizer or antibacterial wipes to easily wash your hands and wipe down any surfaces that may come in contact with your food.

Distance Makes the Stomach Grow Fonder • Sequester raw meat or seafood in its own bag or plastic container, and always transport it to the picnic in a cooler. Be sure to defrost at home, where the temperature is controlled. When barbecuing at the picnic site, keep any plates, cutting boards, or utensils that have met raw meat or fish far, far away from cooked, ready-to-eat foods.

Mayo Maligned • Mayonnaise is not the only culprit for food contamination. Keep mayo-reliant salads and all other dressed, sauced, or prepared foods safe by packing them in a cooler that is below 40°F. (To be OCD about it, you can monitor the temperature by popping a kitchen thermometer into the cooler.)

Time Is Not on Your Side • How long can picnic dishes stay out? Conventional wisdom (aka the F.D.A.) says two hours or so at room temperature, but between 70°F and 117°F (i.e., picnic temp) contaminants multiply much faster. Try to position your spread in the shade, cover exposed bowls and platters, and be sure to return temperature-sensitive food to the cooler after serving.

Don't Crowd • Make sure the items in your cooler have enough breathing room so that the icy air can circulate between them. You can fill the cooler with bagged party ice or, for an even colder option, combine it with dry ice (see page 129). To save on space, use frozen water bottles, which double as beverages once you arrive at the picnic.

When in Doubt, Throw It Out • If a dish seems questionable, choose life over leftovers.

Lyonnaise Potato Salad

Everything there is to adore in this world (bacon, onions, potatoes, eggs, love) goes into this unbeatable potato salad. A play on the classic Lyonnaise-style salad—you know, the one with the poached egg, lardons, and frisée served at French brasseries—it's balanced by a good punch of vinegar to brighten the richness.

SERVES 4 TO 6

- Fine sea salt
- 2 pounds fingerling or baby Yukon Gold potatoes, scrubbed
- 3 tablespoons extra-virgin olive oil
- 4 ounces sliced bacon, cut crosswise into ¼-inch strips
- 1 large shallot, thinly sliced into rings
- ¼ cup red wine vinegar
- 2 teaspoons Dijon mustard
- 1 teaspoon chopped fresh thyme
- Freshly ground pepper
- ⅓ cup chopped fresh flat-leaf parsley
- 1 large egg, hard-cooked (see A Good Egg on page 38) and peeled

IN THE BASKET:

- ☐ Serving spoons

1. Fill a large saucepan two-thirds full of water and season it generously with salt. Quarter the potatoes lengthwise and drop them into the water. Bring to a boil over high heat, then reduce the heat to maintain a gentle simmer and cook until the potatoes are tender but still hold their shape, 8 to 10 minutes.

2. Meanwhile, heat 1 tablespoon of the oil in a sauté pan over medium heat. Add the bacon and sauté until crisp, about 5 minutes. Remove the bacon from the pan with a slotted spoon and transfer it to a small bowl; set aside. Add the shallots to the bacon fat, reduce the heat to medium-low, and sauté until tender, 3 to 5 minutes. Transfer the shallots to the bowl with the bacon. Remove the pan from the heat and whisk the remaining 2 tablespoons oil, the vinegar, mustard, thyme, and pepper into the reserved bacon fat.

3. When the potatoes are done, drain and transfer them to a large bowl along with the bacon and shallots. Drizzle in the dressing (see Tiny Tip) and sprinkle with all but about 2 tablespoons of the parsley (to reserve for garnish). Toss it all together very gently and briefly to avoid mashing the potatoes. Cool

to room temperature, then cover and refrigerate until the picnic, or up to 2 days.

4. Just before the picnic, taste and adjust the seasoning, and add a little more oil if it seems dry. Transfer the salad to a serving bowl. Grate the egg over the salad using the small holes of a box grater. Sprinkle with the reserved parsley and cover to transport to the picnic.

TINY TIP: Don't worry if the potatoes seem overdressed when you toss this salad. You wouldn't believe how much dressing your potatoes are about to absorb in the refrigerator.

The Mile-High Picnic Club

Never go hungry at thirty-three thousand feet again—you can easily pack a crackerjack plane picnic in the time it takes your ride to the airport to arrive. For a morning flight, bring small jars of granola and berries (and ask for milk on the plane), Little Leek and Lancashire Quiches (page 103), or leftover Vanilla Bean Shortcakes (page 138). For an afternoon or evening flight, start with Kale, Sweet Potato, and Goat Cheese Hand Pies (page 105), one of our Ten Best Baguettes (page 98), or a wedge of cheese, sliced salami, and a roll. Add Marcona almonds and dried fruit or small, easy-to-eat fresh fruits like tangerines, sliced apples, or grapes. For dessert, bring a chocolate bar and bonbons. Or, if you're particularly elegant, a box of petits fours. In a show of good olfactory faith to your fellow passengers, stick to snacks that are pleasantly scented (no lutefisk, please).

Japanese Potato Salad

This dish offers the definitive answer to that Thanksgiving imponderable: Why can't we eat mashed potatoes year-round? We can! And in this Japanese twist on potato salad, they're even better by the chilled spoonful. Serve with the Horseradish-Rubbed Flank Steak with Blistered Tomatoes (page 112).

SERVES 4 TO 6

Fine sea salt

2 pounds Yukon Gold potatoes, scrubbed

1 cup D.I.Y. Mayonnaise (page 35) or store-bought, preferably Kewpie brand Japanese mayonnaise

2 tablespoons rice vinegar

2 large carrots, peeled and thinly sliced diagonally

1 cup fresh or frozen shelled edamame

1 Japanese or English cucumber, halved lengthwise and very thinly sliced

4 green onions, white and light green parts only, thinly sliced

IN THE BASKET:

☐ **Serving spoons**

1. Fill a large saucepan two-thirds full with water and season generously with salt. Peel the potatoes, cut them into 2-inch chunks, and drop them into the water. Bring the water to a boil over high heat, then reduce the heat to maintain a gentle simmer and cook until the potatoes are very tender, 10 to 15 minutes. Drain in a colander and set aside for 5 minutes to steam dry. While the potatoes are still hot, mash them using a ricer, food mill, or potato masher. Add the mayonnaise, vinegar, and ½ teaspoon salt to the warm potatoes and whip with a wooden spoon until light and fluffy. Set aside to cool.

2. Meanwhile, fill a small saucepan with water, season it generously with salt, and bring it to a boil over high heat. Add the carrots and edamame and cook until crisp-tender, about 3 minutes. Drain, rinse under cold water, and dry well.

3. Put the cucumbers in a bowl and sprinkle with ½ teaspoon salt. Toss to coat evenly and set aside for 15 minutes. Wrap the cucumbers in a kitchen towel or paper towels and squeeze out as much liquid as you can.

4. Add the cucumbers, carrots, edamame, and green onions to the cooled potato mixture and stir to combine well. Taste and adjust the seasoning. Cover and refrigerate until the picnic, or for up to 2 days. Just before leaving for the picnic, transfer the salad to a serving bowl and cover tightly for transport.

CHAPTER 4

Plates

Every picnic should feature a showstopper, and these protein-packed mains are ready for the spotlight. Impress your fellow guests by bringing indoor splendor to the great outdoors with a jaw-dropping platter of Horseradish-Rubbed Flank Steak with Blistered Tomatoes (page 112), a stunning side of Cold Poached Salmon with Green Goddess Sauce (page 116), or a flavor-packed Roast Pork with Watercress and Green Garlic Salsa Verde (page 118). These dishes are decisively suited to being served at room temperature, but since some like it hot, remember that packing entrees in your wheelie cooler helps them maintain their original temperature.

Postcard Pissaladière

A trip to Provence landed us this melt-in-your-mouth onion tart (pronounced *peace-a-la-dee-yair*) featuring an ultraflaky, free-form crust topped with meltingly soft and sweet onions, anchovies, and Niçoise olives. It's best served at room temperature a few hours after baking.

SERVES 8 TO 12

1 cup all-purpose flour, plus more for rolling the dough

1½ teaspoons fine sea salt

10 tablespoons cold unsalted butter, cubed

3 to 4 tablespoons ice-cold water

2 tablespoons extra-virgin olive oil

2 pounds sweet yellow onions (about 3 medium), thinly sliced

Freshly ground pepper

10 oil-packed anchovy fillets, drained

⅓ cup pitted Niçoise or other small black olives

IN THE BASKET:

- ☐ **Knife**
- ☐ **Pastry server**

❶ Put the flour and ½ teaspoon of the salt in the bowl of a food processor and pulse just to blend. Add the butter and pulse until the mixture is about the size of grains of rice. With the motor running, drizzle in cold water through the feed tube until the dough looks moist and clumps together easily. Spread a large piece of plastic wrap out on a countertop and dump the dough into the center. Wrap it up tightly in the plastic, pressing and molding it into a solid disk. Refrigerate for about 1 hour.

❷ Meanwhile, heat the oil over medium heat in a large Dutch oven or other heavy pot. Add the onions and the remaining 1 teaspoon salt and stir to coat with oil. Cover and cook, stirring once or twice, until the onions are softened and translucent, about 20 minutes (see Tiny Tip). Reduce the heat to low and continue cooking, covered, until they are meltingly soft but not browned, about 40 minutes more, stirring every 10 minutes or so. Remove the lid and increase the heat to medium-high to evaporate most of the liquid, 6 to 8 minutes. Season with salt and pepper.

❸ Preheat the oven to 375°F about 20 minutes before shaping the crust.

4. Place the dough on a generously floured countertop and use a floured rolling pin to roll it out into a large circle about ⅛ inch thick. Loosely roll the dough up on the rolling pin, then unroll it onto a large ungreased baking sheet. Fold in about ½ inch of dough around the edges to form a double-thick crust, and crimp the edges with your floured thumb and forefinger or with the tines of a fork.

5. Spread the onion mixture evenly over the pastry. Arrange the anchovy fillets over the onions in a pretty pattern, such as wheel spokes or latticework. Complete your design by dotting the tart with the olives.

6. Bake until the edges are golden and crisp, 30 to 35 minutes, rotating the pan halfway through. Completely cool the tart on the baking sheet. Cut it into wedges or squares, or wait and do this at the picnic site. Wrap the tart tightly with foil to transport.

TINY TIP: The onions are not caramelized in this tart, but cooked gently, which makes them incomparably sweet and silky. Resist the temptation to rush this step—just let them do their thing.

Ten Best Baguettes

The iconic baguette anchors a picnic-proof sandwich—its hardy crust protects whatever gourmet goods you stuff inside. Bring it to the blanket whole and slice it to serve any number of picnickers, or prepare individual servings in advance by cutting the baguette into 6-inch lengths and wrapping each with parchment paper.

Grilled Broccolini + Aioli (page 35) + Avocado + Chile Flakes + Lemon Juice

Tuna + Tomatoes + Lettuce + Hard-Cooked Eggs + Olives + Anchovies

Ham + Gruyère + Dijon + Butter

Strawberries + Camembert

Roasted Eggplant + Harissa + Labneh + Pickled Red Onions (see You Can Pickle That on page 60)

Coronation Chicken (page 124) + Butter Lettuce + Toasted Flaked Coconut

Turkey + Triple Crème + Apricot Jam

Country Pork Pâté + D.I.Y. Mayonnaise (page 35); Quickle Pickle Rainbow Carrots (page 60) + Cilantro + Sliced Jalapeño

Egg Salad (page 34) + Pickled Shallots (see You Can Pickle That on page 60) + Watercress

Roast Beef + Green Garlic Salsa Verde (page 119)

Za'atar Lamb Meatball Pitas

The Mediterranean spice blend za'atar is magic in these oven-baked lamb meatballs, packed snugly into pitas with tomatoes and cucumbers. You could purchase premade za'atar in the spice aisle at a specialty store, but it's best to mix it yourself and include fresh herbs.

SERVES 6

Yogurt Sauce

1 cup Greek-style yogurt

2 tablespoons fresh lemon juice

¼ cup finely chopped fresh mint

¼ teaspoon fine sea salt

¼ teaspoon freshly ground pepper

Za'atar

1 tablespoon sesame seeds

1 tablespoon sumac

1 tablespoon ground cumin

1 tablespoon minced fresh thyme

1 tablespoon minced fresh oregano

1 teaspoon fine sea salt

1 teaspoon freshly ground pepper

Lamb Meatball Pitas

1 pound ground lamb

¼ cup minced fresh mint, plus additional leaves for garnish

One batch za'atar (see above)

2 tablespoons finely grated red onion

2 garlic cloves, minced

1 teaspoon fine sea salt

3 pocket-style pitas

2 tomatoes, cored, halved, and cut into ¼-inch slices

½ cucumber, halved lengthwise and cut into ¼-inch slices

½ red onion, finely diced

1. To make the yogurt sauce: Whisk together the yogurt, lemon juice, mint, salt, and pepper. Cover and refrigerate for up to 4 days.

2. To make the za'atar: Swirl the sesame seeds in a small pan over medium heat until toasted. Combine the sesame seeds, sumac, cumin, thyme, oregano, salt, and pepper in a small bowl.

3. To make the lamb meatball pitas: Preheat the oven to 500°F. Combine the lamb, mint, za'atar, grated onion, garlic, and salt in a mixing bowl. Roll the mixture into eighteen 1-inch (about 1-ounce) meatballs, placing them at least 1 inch apart on a rimmed baking sheet. Bake until cooked through, about 8 minutes. Place under the broiler to brown, about 2 minutes. Transfer to a plate lined with a paper towel to cool.

4. Toast the pitas lightly in a toaster or in a 350°F oven. Slice them in half and open up the pockets (see Tiny Tip). Place three meatballs and alternating slices of tomato and cucumber inside each pita. Sprinkle with the diced onion and garnish with mint leaves. Store the pitas in a shallow dish and cover for transport. At the picnic, invite guests to spoon yogurt sauce atop their pitas.

TINY TIP: For a speedy assembly line, immediately place a cold egg inside each hot pita as a placeholder. When they cool, they will be permanently popped open and easy to fill.

IN THE BASKET:

- ☐ Yogurt sauce + spoon

Mini Pita Variation

To convert this recipe into an hors d'oeuvre, stuff 18 mini pocket pitas with a single meatball, 1 slice of tomato, and 2 slices of cucumber. Garnish each pita with a dollop of yogurt sauce and a mint sprig.

Menu: Meet Me at the Manor

Tarts and sandies rendezvous in the English countryside.

Savory Rosemary Pecan Sandies with Marmalade 48

Asparagus and Fava Beans with Poppy Seed Vinaigrette 80

Little Leek and Lancashire Quiches 103

Coronation Chicken in Lettuce Cups 124

Petite Pavlovas with Limey Roasted Rhubarb 144

Elderflower Pimm's Cups 173

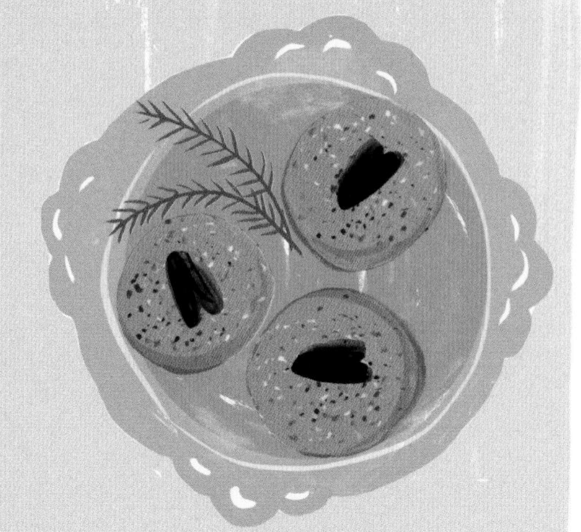

Little Leek and Lancashire Quiches

Bake these individual quiches in a regular muffin tin, which doubles as a carrier, or use 4-ounce ramekins if you're packing just a few. Serve with salad greens tossed with Shallot Shake-Up Vinaigrette (page 71).

MAKES 12

- 4 medium leeks
- 3 tablespoons unsalted butter
- 2 teaspoons chopped fresh thyme
- 1 teaspoon fine sea salt
- Freshly ground pepper
- 4 large eggs
- 2 large egg yolks
- 2/3 cup sour cream
- 1/2 cup whole milk
- 2 cups shredded Lancashire cheese, or other sharp white Cheddar
- Flour for dusting
- One 17.3-ounce package puff pastry (2 sheets), thawed according to package directions

IN THE BASKET:

- ☐ **Salad greens**
- ☐ **Salad servers**
- ☐ **Shallot Shake-Up Vinaigrette**

1. Position a rack in the center of the oven and preheat it to 400°F. Have ready a standard 12-cup muffin tin.

2. Trim the roots and dark green tops from the leeks. Halve them lengthwise, then thinly slice crosswise. Put the sliced leeks in a large bowl and fill it with cold water. Swish the leeks around to remove any sand or dirt. The leeks will float to the surface of the water and the dirt will fall to the bottom; skim the leeks from the top and transfer to a salad spinner or kitchen towel and dry.

3. Melt the butter in a large sauté pan over medium heat. Add the leeks and sauté until very soft and the liquid they release has evaporated, 6 to 8 minutes. Decrease the heat to medium-low and continue cooking until the leeks are falling-apart tender and some are light golden brown, 7 to 10 minutes. Stir in the thyme, salt, and a pinch of pepper, and cook about 1 minute more. Remove the pan from the heat and set aside to cool.

4. Whisk together the eggs, yolks, sour cream, and milk in a large bowl. Stir in the leeks and about half of the cheese; set aside.

Continued

5. On a lightly floured countertop, roll out one of the puff pastry sheets to a 13½-by-9-inch rectangle about ⅛ inch thick. Cut the rectangle into 6 squares, then line 6 of the cups in the muffin tin with a square of pastry, allowing the corners to overhang. Repeat with the remaining sheet of pastry, lining the other 6 cups of the tin. Fill the puff pastry cups with the leek mixture, dividing it evenly. They should be quite full, but not so full that they overflow. Sprinkle the tops with the remaining cheese.

6. Bake until the pastry is deep golden brown and the tops are lightly browned, about 30 minutes, rotating the pan about halfway through for even cooking. Cool for about 5 minutes, then run a dull knife around the edges of each muffin cup to release the quiche. Leave them in the muffin tin to transport to the picnic, or transfer to a platter. Serve warm or at room temperature within 4 hours.

Kale, Sweet Potato, and Goat Cheese Hand Pies

Pacific Pie Company owner Sarah Curtis-Fawley forever delights us with her attractive and savory hand pies. Serve these pasties warm or at room temperature, and if you need a plan-ahead pie, make them on a Sunday afternoon and freeze them for up to a month.

MAKES 12

- 1 batch Perfect Pie Dough, chilled (recipe follows)
- 1¼ pounds sweet potatoes, peeled and cut into ½-inch chunks
- 3 tablespoons olive oil
- ¾ teaspoon plus ½ teaspoon fine sea salt
- 1 teaspoon freshly ground pepper
- 1 tablespoon unsalted butter
- 2 medium yellow onions, halved and thinly sliced
- 1 bunch lacinato or Tuscan kale, stemmed and coarsely chopped
- 3 garlic cloves, minced
- 1 tablespoon balsamic vinegar
- ½ teaspoon dried red pepper flakes
- 4 ounces goat cheese, crumbled
- Heavy cream or melted butter, for brushing

IN THE BASKET:

- ☐ **Napkins**
- ☐ **Platter**

1. Preheat the oven to 375°F.
2. Cut the chilled disk of pie dough into 12 wedges. One at a time, roll each wedge into a ball, then use a rolling pin to roll the dough into a 4-inch round on a lightly floured countertop. Separate the rounds with pieces of parchment paper, stack them on a plate, and chill in the refrigerator for at least 10 minutes before filling.
3. To make the filling: Toss the sweet potatoes with 1 tablespoon of the oil and sprinkle them with ¾ teaspoon salt and ½ teaspoon of the pepper. Arrange the sweet potatoes in a single layer on a baking sheet and roast until just starting to brown, 30 to 40 minutes.
4. Meanwhile, heat the remaining 2 tablespoons oil and the butter in a large sauté pan over medium heat. Add the onions and sauté until deep golden brown, lowering the heat as needed if they begin to burn, 30 to 40 minutes. Add the kale, garlic, vinegar, dried red pepper, and the remaining ½ teaspoon each of salt and pepper and cook until the kale is wilted, 3 to 5 minutes.

Continued

5. Scrape the kale mixture into a large bowl and gently stir in the roasted sweet potatoes. Chill the filling mixture until cold before making the hand pies, about 2 hours, or for up to 2 days.

6. To make the hand pies: Lay the chilled pastry rounds on a countertop. Using a pastry brush, lightly brush the outside edges with water. Put ¼ cup of the filling on one half of each pastry circle, leaving a ½-inch border. Top each with crumbled cheese. Fold the pastry over to cover the filling and press the edges together firmly to seal. Decoratively crimp the crust by pinching it at even intervals, or press with the tines of a fork to seal, then trim any uneven edges with a knife. Using the tip of a knife, cut three small slits in the top of each pie.

7. Arrange the pies on a baking sheet at least 1 inch apart and chill for at least 1 hour, or for up to 1 day, covered. (The pies can also be wrapped individually in aluminum foil and placed in the freezer for up to 1 month; do not defrost before baking, but increase the baking time as needed.) Preheat the oven to 375°F shortly before taking the pies from the refrigerator.

8. Lightly brush the pies with cream or melted butter. Bake the pies until golden brown, 30 to 40 minutes. Cool the pies on a wire rack, and arrange them on a platter.

Variation

To make a sweet hand pie, substitute Peachy Keen Mason Jar Pie filling (page 156) for the savory filling in this pie.

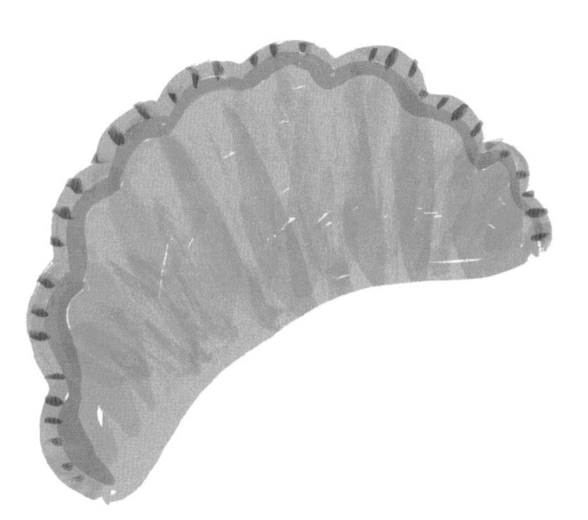

Perfect Pie Dough

MAKES A SINGLE 9-INCH CRUST

10 tablespoons (1¼ sticks) cold unsalted butter

1½ cups all-purpose flour, plus more for dusting

½ teaspoon fine sea salt

6 to 8 tablespoons ice-cold water

1. Cube the butter, put it in a small bowl, and place it in the freezer until firm and very cold, about 10 minutes. Put the flour, salt, and chilled butter in a food processor and pulse until the butter chunks are the size of peas. Add half of the cold water and process very briefly, then add the remaining water 1 tablespoon at a time, pulsing between additions, just until large moist clumps form.

2. Transfer the dough to a lightly floured countertop and, using the heel of your hand, smear the clumps of dough until they come together. Use a pastry scraper to form the dough into a mound, then gently pat it into a disk. Wrap tightly in plastic and refrigerate for at least 30 minutes, or up to 2 days. To freeze, wrap it in another layer of plastic and freeze for up to 3 months.

Blue Ribbon Tomato Pie

Stick to Early Girls or Romas for this recipe; juicy tomatoes, while perfect for snacking, make for a soggy slice of pie.

SERVES 8

Crust

1 cup all-purpose flour, plus more for rolling the dough

½ cup cornmeal, preferably finely ground

½ teaspoon fine sea salt

6 tablespoons cold unsalted butter, cubed

¼ cup plus 1 tablespoon cold buttermilk

Filling

2 pounds ripe, firm tomatoes, such as Early Girls or Romas, cored and cut into ¼-inch slices)

1 teaspoon fine sea salt

½ cup D.I.Y. Mayonnaise (page 35) or store-bought mayonnaise

¼ cup drained diced pimento peppers, roasted red bell peppers, or piquillo peppers

1 green onion, white and green parts, thinly sliced

½ teaspoon freshly ground pepper

2½ cups grated extra-sharp Cheddar

¼ cup finely grated Parmigiano-Reggiano

1½ tablespoons cornmeal

IN THE BASKET:

- ☐ **Knife**
- ☐ **Pastry server**

1. To make the crust: Put the flour, cornmeal, and salt in a food processor and pulse to combine. Add the butter and pulse a few times until the largest chunks are the size of peas. With the motor running, drizzle in ¼ cup of the buttermilk and process just until large, moist clumps form; if the dough is too dry to come together, add the remaining 1 tablespoon buttermilk. Spread a large piece of plastic wrap out on a countertop and dump the clumpy dough in the center. Gather the edges of the plastic and use them to press the dough into a flat, cohesive disk. Chill for at least 1 hour.

2. To make the filling: Line a baking sheet with a double thickness of paper towels. Spread the tomatoes in a single layer on the paper towels and sprinkle with the salt. Set aside for about 1 hour for the tomatoes to give up their juice.

3. Whisk together the mayonnaise, pimento peppers, green onion, and pepper in a medium bowl. Mix the cheeses together in a separate bowl. Reserve ¼ cup of the cheese mixture and add the rest to the mayonnaise. Stir together.

4. Preheat the oven to 400°F about 30 minutes before you plan to bake.

5. Roll out the dough on a lightly floured surface to a 12-inch circle. Loosely roll the dough up onto the rolling pin, then unroll it into a deep 9-inch pie dish. Gently press the dough into the corners of the dish. Fold the overhanging edges under to create a double-thick crust lining the rim of the dish. Crimp the crust by pinching the dough together with your thumb and index finger at even intervals, creating peaks and valleys. If the dough is a bit sticky, dip your fingers in flour as you go.

6. Sprinkle cornmeal evenly over the bottom of the crust. Arrange a third of the tomatoes over the cornmeal, overlapping as needed. Top with half of the pimento cheese, spreading it in an even layer to the edges. Repeat layering with half of the remaining tomatoes and all the remaining pimento cheese. Finish with the remaining tomato slices and sprinkle the top with the reserved cheese mixture.

7. Bake until the crust and cheese are golden brown, 35 to 40 minutes (check the crust halfway and tent with foil if it's getting too dark). Cool the pie for at least 1 hour before slicing and serving. It is delicious served warm or at room temperature.

Vietnamese Noodle Bowls
with Shrimp and Vegetables

Serve these fresh, healthful noodles in takeout boxes with chopsticks. (Just pop into your local Chinese restaurant and ask to buy a few extras.) Bring Vietnam's staple fish sauce, nuoc cham, to serve on the side. You can dress the salad in advance, but taste as you go to make sure it's not too spicy; nuoc cham means business.

SERVES 4 TO 6

- 12 to 18 large shrimp, peeled, tail intact
- 2 lemongrass stalks
- 2 tablespoons Vietnamese fish sauce
- 2 tablespoons sugar
- 1 tablespoon minced garlic
- 3 tablespoons vegetable or other neutral oil, plus more for brushing the grill
- 12 ounces dried rice vermicelli noodles
- 2 cups thinly sliced green cabbage
- 2 large carrots, peeled and cut into matchsticks
- 1 small cucumber, quartered lengthwise and thinly sliced crosswise
- ⅓ cup coarsely chopped cashews
- ⅓ cup coarsely chopped fresh cilantro
- ⅓ cup coarsely chopped fresh mint

Nuoc Cham Sauce

- ⅓ cup Vietnamese fish sauce
- ¼ cup sugar
- 2 tablespoons minced garlic
- ¼ cup fresh lime juice
- 2 or more red or green Thai chiles, stemmed and thinly sliced
- 2 tablespoons water

1. Butterfly the shrimp by cutting a deep slit down the back of each one, all the way from the base of the tail to the head, taking care not to cut all the way through. Remove the vein and spread the shrimp open so they lie flat.

2. Trim the green tops and hard root ends from the lemongrass and peel away the tough outer layers. Finely mince the tender, innermost parts of the stalks. Mix the lemongrass with the fish sauce, sugar, garlic, and 1 tablespoon of the oil in a medium bowl, stirring to dissolve the sugar. Add the shrimp and toss to coat. Cover and refrigerate for 30 minutes.

3. Meanwhile, submerge the noodles in a bowl of lukewarm water and let stand until pliable, about 30 minutes.

4. Bring a large pot of water to a boil over high heat. Drain the softened noodles and add them to the pot. Cook until al dente, which may take from 30 seconds to 3 minutes, depending on the brand of noodles. Drain the noodles in a colander under cold running water. Drain well and transfer to a large bowl. Add the

remaining 2 tablespoons oil and toss to coat. Add the cabbage, carrots, and cucumber and mix it all together. Divide the noodles among individual containers.

5. Prepare a hot fire in a charcoal or gas grill, or heat a grill pan over high heat and brush it lightly with oil.

6. Remove the shrimp from the marinade and shake off any excess. Grill the shrimp until pink and lightly charred, 1 to 2 minutes per side. Cool for about 10 minutes, then divide the shrimp among the containers. Top with the cashews, cilantro, and mint, cover the containers, and pack them into the picnic basket at once or refrigerate for up to 4 hours.

7. To make the nuoc cham: Combine the fish sauce, sugar, garlic, lime juice, chiles, and water in a small jar with a tight-fitting lid or a squeeze bottle. Shake or stir the mixture until the sugar is dissolved. Refrigerate for up to 5 days. Serve at the picnic site for drizzling over the noodles.

IN THE BASKET:

- ☐ **Nuoc cham**
- ☐ **Chopsticks**

Horseradish-Rubbed Flank Steak
with Blistered Tomatoes

As picnic-ready cuts of beef go, flank steak tops our list. It's affordable, it cooks quickly, and it has a delicious flavor and tender texture when served at room temperature.

SERVES 4 TO 6

¼ cup prepared horseradish (about half a 4-ounce jar)

4 garlic cloves, finely minced

1 tablespoon extra-virgin olive oil, plus more for drizzling

1 tablespoon dark brown sugar

1 tablespoon fine sea salt plus more for sprinkling

1 teaspoon freshly cracked pepper

One 2-pound flank steak

1½ pounds cherry or cocktail tomatoes on the vine

IN THE BASKET:

- ☐ **Steak knives**

1. Whisk together the horseradish, garlic, oil, sugar, salt, and pepper in a small bowl. Lay the steak in a baking dish and rub it with the marinade, coating all sides. Cover and chill for 2 hours to marinate, or for up to 1 day.

2. Prepare a hot fire in a charcoal or gas grill. Wipe the excess marinade from the steak. Grill until the steak is medium-rare in the middle, 4 to 5 minutes per side. Transfer the steak to a cutting board to rest for at least 10 minutes. Or refrigerate until the picnic, or up to 2 days.

3. While the steak is resting, drizzle the tomatoes with oil and a pinch of salt, but keep them connected to the vines. Carefully place the tomatoes on the grill. Close the lid and cook until softened, wilted, and lightly charred, 10 to 15 minutes.

4. Just before leaving for the picnic, slice the steak against the grain into thick strips and transfer them to a serving platter. Top with the tomato vines, drizzle with a little more oil, and cover tightly for transport.

Menu: Belles with Baskets

Court the Carolinas in this celebration of all things south of the Mason-Dixon line.

Smoky Tea–Brined Fried Chicken

This chicken is delicious on its own, but even better with a batch of homemade Quickle Pickles (page 59) and Candy-Striped Beet, Fennel, and Apple Coleslaw (page 82).

SERVES 4 TO 6

Brine

1 quart tepid water

½ cup fine sea salt

¼ cup honey

Zest of 1 large orange, removed in large strips with a vegetable peeler

¼ cup lapsang souchong, or other smoked tea

1 quart ice water

Chicken

One 3- to 4-pound chicken, cut into 10 pieces (breasts halved), backbone discarded

3 cups all-purpose flour

1 cup fine cornmeal

2 tablespoons Old Bay or Cajun seasoning

2 teaspoons kosher or fine sea salt

½ teaspoon freshly ground black pepper

1 cup buttermilk

Peanut or vegetable oil, for frying

IN THE BASKET:

- ☐ **Serving tongs**
- ☐ **Moist towelettes**

1. For the brine: Combine the tepid water, salt, honey, and zest in a large pot. Bring to a boil over high heat, stirring to dissolve, then turn off the heat and stir in the tea. Steep for 5 minutes. Pour the brine through a mesh strainer into a large bowl or container; discard the solids. Add the ice water and cool completely. Submerge the chicken pieces in the brine, cover, and refrigerate for 4 to 6 hours.

2. Remove the chicken from the brine, rinse, and pat dry; discard the brine. Let the chicken sit at room temperature for about 30 minutes.

3. Meanwhile, put 1 cup of the flour in a large bowl. Combine the remaining 2 cups flour with the cornmeal, Old Bay, salt, and pepper in another large bowl. Pour the buttermilk into a third bowl. Set up a breading station in the following order: flour, buttermilk, cornmeal coating. Dip each piece of chicken into the flour, shaking off the excess, then into the buttermilk, then into the cornmeal coating, patting it in so that it adheres well.

4. Pour oil into a 10- to 12-inch cast-iron skillet or other heavy straight-sided skillet to a depth of ¾ inch. Heat the oil over high heat until a

deep-frying thermometer registers 350°F. Line a large tray with paper towels to collect the chicken after it is fried.

5. When the oil has reached the proper temperature, carefully lower in several pieces of chicken, but avoid crowding or overflowing the oil. The temperature will decrease, so leave the heat on high until it returns to 350°F, then adjust the heat as necessary to maintain that temperature. Fry the chicken until deep golden brown and a thermometer inserted into the thickest part of each piece registers 165°F to 170°F, turning once or twice, 12 to 16 minutes. Let cooked pieces rest on the prepared tray. Repeat to fry the remaining chicken.

6. Take the chicken to the picnic at once, or cool to room temperature, then refrigerate up to 24 hours and serve cool at the picnic.

Cold Poached Salmon
with Green Goddess Sauce

If you want to be the one who arrives bearing the picnic's pièce de résistance, this stunning slab of salmon is your Mona Lisa.

SERVES 6 TO 8

2 celery ribs, cut into ½-inch slices

2 large carrots, cut into ½-inch slices

2 large leeks, white and green parts, cut into ½-inch slices and washed well

4 garlic cloves, smashed

5 or 6 fresh parsley sprigs

3 or 4 fresh thyme sprigs

10 black peppercorns

1 bay leaf

3 lemons, 2 halved and 1 very thinly sliced into rounds

1½ cups dry white wine

¾ cup white wine vinegar

One 2½- to 3-pound side of salmon, pin bones removed

Fine sea salt

6 cups lightly packed baby arugula

1 cucumber, very thinly sliced

Green Goddess Sauce (recipe follows)

IN THE BASKET:

- ☐ **Green Goddess Sauce + small spoon**
- ☐ **Knife + pastry server**

1. Put the celery, carrots, leeks, garlic, parsley, thyme, peppercorns, and bay leaf in a fish poacher or a large roasting pan. Pour in 8 to 12 cups of water, to cover the vegetables by at least 1 inch. Place the pan over medium-high heat and bring to a gentle boil. Add the lemon halves, wine, and vinegar.

2. Season the salmon with salt, then lower it into the pan, skin side down, and rest it on the vegetables. Add water if the salmon is not completely submerged. Bring the liquid back up to around 190°F and adjust the heat to maintain that temperature while poaching.

3. Remove the pan from the heat when the thickest part of the fillet reaches 100°F, 6 to 10 minutes. Leave the salmon in the liquid to cool for about 1 hour, then refrigerate until cold, at least 2 hours, or for up to 1 day.

4. Before the picnic, line a platter with the lemon slices around the edge. Mound the arugula on the platter. Use the largest spatulas you have to gently lift the salmon from the poaching liquid. Drain well and place on the platter. (Strain and reserve the poaching liquid; it freezes well.) Cover the surface of the salmon with the cucumber slices, overlapping them like fish scales. Wrap the platter tightly with plastic wrap and transport to the picnic. Cut slices and serve with the sauce spooned over the top.

Green Goddess Sauce

MAKES $2\frac{1}{4}$ CUPS

- $\frac{3}{4}$ cup mayonnaise
- 1 cup fresh flat-leaf parsley leaves
- 1 cup tarragon leaves (one $\frac{3}{4}$-ounce package)
- 4 green onions, white and light green parts, coarsely chopped
- 2 oil-packed anchovy fillets, drained
- 1 garlic clove, smashed
- 3 tablespoons tarragon vinegar
- $1\frac{1}{2}$ teaspoons fine sea salt
- $\frac{1}{2}$ teaspoon freshly ground pepper
- $\frac{3}{4}$ cup sour cream

Combine the mayonnaise, parsley, tarragon, onions, anchovies, garlic, vinegar, salt, and pepper in a blender and process until smooth. Add the sour cream and blend just until combined. Taste and adjust the seasoning. Refrigerate until the picnic, or for up to 3 days.

Roast Pork with Watercress
and Green Garlic Salsa Verde

Nothing heralds the onset of picnic season like seeing the first bunches of green garlic at the farmers' market. These grassy green stalks, which come from the young garlic plant before cloves form, are more subdued than their bulbous brethren, but impart incredible flavor. If you can't track it down, substitute regular garlic.

SERVES 4 TO 6

2 teaspoons fennel seeds
¾ teaspoon black peppercorns
2 teaspoons fine sea salt
1½ teaspoons sugar
One 1½-pound boneless pork loin roast
1½ tablespoons olive oil, plus more for rubbing the pork
3 bunches watercress, trimmed, leaving at least 1 inch of stem intact
Green Garlic Salsa Verde (recipe follows)

IN THE BASKET:

- ☐ **Green Garlic Salsa Verde + spoon**
- ☐ **Serving tongs**

1. Crush the fennel seeds and peppercorns to a powder with a mortar and pestle or spice grinder, then mix with the salt and sugar in a small bowl. Rub the seasoning mix all over the pork to coat well. Set aside for 1 hour at room temperature or, preferably, cover loosely and refrigerate overnight. If refrigerated, remove the pork about 1 hour before roasting so that it comes to room temperature.

2. Position a rack in the center of the oven and preheat it to 275°F. Pat the pork dry with paper towels, then rub it with olive oil to coat all sides.

3. Heat a large ovenproof skillet, preferably cast iron, over high heat until smoking-hot, then add the 1½ tablespoons of oil. When you just begin to see wisps of smoke, add the pork, fat side down first, and sear until golden brown on all sides, 2 to 3 minutes per side. Reduce the heat to medium-high if it appears to be burning before forming a brown crust. Transfer the skillet to the oven and roast until a thermometer registers 145°F in the center of the

meat, about 20 minutes. Rest the roast out of the oven 15 to 30 minutes before slicing, or cool to room temperature and refrigerate it (unsliced) for up to 2 days.

4. Slice the roast pork against the grain as thinly as you can. Pile the watercress in the center of a large platter and fan the sliced pork over the top; cover tightly with plastic wrap. At the picnic site, spoon the salsa verde over the pork before serving.

Green Garlic Salsa Verde

MAKES ABOUT 1 CUP

- One 2-inch piece green garlic, white and light green part only, or 1 large garlic clove
- ½ cup lightly packed mixed fresh tender herbs, such as sprigs of dill, tarragon, and fennel fronds, and snipped chives
- ¼ cup lightly packed fresh flat-leaf parsley leaves
- ¼ cup lightly packed fresh mint leaves
- ½ cup extra-virgin olive oil
- 2 tablespoons red wine vinegar
- 2 tablespoons capers, drained and rinsed
- 1 teaspoon fine sea salt

Put the green garlic, mixed herbs, parsley, and mint in a food processor and process until finely minced. Transfer the mixture to a bowl and stir in the oil, vinegar, capers, and salt. The flavor will develop over time, so cover and let sit at least 30 minutes, or refrigerate for up to 3 days. (The olive oil will rise to the top and prevent the herbs from browning.)

Muffuletta Pressed Sandwich

Smoosh this decadent New Orleans sandwich into a biteable bonanza with the help of a heavy picnic basket, or 100 copies of this cookbook.

SERVES 4 TO 6

Olive Salad

2 cups Quickle Pickle Giardiniera (page 61), drained

1 cup green olives, drained and pitted

1 cup Kalamata or oil-cured black olives, drained and pitted

3 tablespoons capers, drained and rinsed

2/3 cup extra-virgin olive oil

Sandwich

One 8-by-12-inch focaccia slab

4 ounces thinly sliced mortadella

3 ounces thinly sliced provolone

4 ounces thinly sliced salami

3 ounces thinly sliced Swiss cheese

4 ounces thinly sliced ham

IN THE BASKET:

- ☐ Serrated knife
- ☐ Cutting board

1. To make the olive salad: Pulse the giardiniera, green and black olives, and capers together in a food processor until coarsely chopped. Stir the oil into the mixture, cover, and refrigerate overnight, or up to 1 week.

2. To make the sandwich: Halve the bread lengthwise and spread 1 cup of the olive salad on each side. Build the sandwich by alternating layers of meat and cheese in the following order: mortadella, provolone, salami, Swiss, ham. Wrap the sandwich in plastic and place it between two baking sheets weighted with a picnic basket for at least 1 hour.

3. At the picnic, unwrap and cut the pressed sandwich into squares.

Behold, the Picnic Buffet

On very few occasions, usually involving sand—e.g., a lobster boil, a crab feast, an oyster bake—it's best to move your picnic to a table. The rest of the time, it's much more fun to lay a blanket on a lush lawn and forgo the propriety of chairs. But even if you'd rather not sit at a picnic table, it can come in handy as a ready buffet, providing an attractive display for your manifold menu while also preventing spills. Place silverware, napkins, and plates at one end of the table. Set a showstopper, like an oversize charcuterie board or eye-catching whole-poached salmon, as a central focal point. Then create a progressive spread that moves from bites to salads to plates and sweets. (For the most attractive array, vary the heights and shapes of the serveware, placing dissimilar items next to each other.) Set glasses and sips at the end of the table, after the sweets, so your picnickers have a free hand to pick up their pretties as they work their way down the table. If the picnic is a manageable size, ask each cook to introduce her dish, so that guests with food restrictions know what to watch for. If the picnic is enormous—such as a school fair or a block party—bring place cards and ask each guest to write a description of the dish next to her serving platter. And, no matter the size of the picnic, tuck a few extra serving spoons in your picnic basket. Even avid picnickers are apt to forget them.

Brick-Roasted Chicken
with Zucchini and Apricot Couscous

Chicken al mattone, or "brick chicken," is a Tuscan technique for cooking a butterflied chicken under the weight of a brick, or a heavy cast-iron skillet. This technique cooks the chicken evenly and quickly.

SERVES 4 TO 6

Chicken

1 teaspoon ground coriander

1 teaspoon ground cumin

1 teaspoon fine sea salt

½ teaspoon freshly ground pepper

One 3- to 4-pound chicken, backbone removed, rinsed and patted dry

2 tablespoons extra-virgin olive oil, plus more for greasing the brick

Couscous

1½ cups homemade or low-sodium store-bought chicken stock

Finely grated zest and juice of 1 large orange

2 garlic cloves, coarsely chopped

1 teaspoon fine sea salt

½ teaspoon black peppercorns

½ teaspoon coriander

½ teaspoon cumin

1¼ cups couscous, preferably whole wheat

1 small zucchini, cut lengthwise into 8 spears and thinly sliced crosswise into small triangles

⅓ cup finely chopped unsulfured dried apricots

2 tablespoons chopped fresh cilantro

2 tablespoons chopped fresh mint

2 lemons, cut into wedges

1. To roast the chicken: Stir together the coriander, cumin, salt, and pepper in a small bowl. Invert the chicken to pop out the sternum so it lies flat. Place it skin side up, in a large baking dish. Sprinkle the spice mixture evenly over both sides of the chicken. Loosely cover and refrigerate overnight, or for up to 2 days.

2. Remove the chicken from the refrigerator about 30 minutes before roasting. Position a rack in the center of the oven and preheat it to 400°F. Wrap a brick in aluminum foil and grease it with oil, or grease the bottom of a small heavy skillet.

3. Heat the oil in a large cast-iron skillet over medium-high heat. When you just begin to see wisps of smoke, add the chicken, skin side down, and cook until golden brown, about 5 minutes. Place the brick on top of the chicken and transfer it to the oven. Roast until the skin is deeply browned, about 30 minutes. Remove the brick, turn the chicken over, and place the brick back on top. Continue roasting until a thermometer registers 165°F in the thickest part of the thigh and the juices run clear, 10 to 15 minutes more. Transfer the chicken to a

cutting board to rest for 20 minutes. Reserve the pan drippings.

4. To carve, remove the leg-thigh pieces from the body and separate them. Halve the bird between the breasts, then cut the breasts in half. Leave the wings attached to half of each breast or separate them.

5. To make the couscous: Slowly bring the stock, orange zest and juice, garlic, salt, peppercorns, coriander, and cumin to a boil over medium heat in a small saucepan.

6. Meanwhile, toss the couscous, zucchini, and dried apricots together in a large heatproof bowl, and set a fine-mesh strainer nearby. When the liquid reaches a boil, pour it through the strainer into the bowl; discard the solids. Make sure everything in the bowl is submerged, then immediately cover it tightly with plastic wrap. Set aside to steam until the liquid is absorbed, 5 to 7 minutes.

7. Uncover the bowl and use a fork to fluff the couscous. Drizzle with 2 tablespoons to ¼ cup of the chicken pan juices, and gently toss to mix. Taste and adjust the seasoning, then set aside to cool for up to 2 hours before the picnic, or refrigerate for up to 1 day.

8. Just before the picnic, toss the cilantro and mint into the couscous. Pour the couscous into the center of a large rimmed platter and top with the chicken pieces. Put the lemons around the edges and cover tightly for transport.

IN THE BASKET:

- ☐ **Serving fork + spoon**

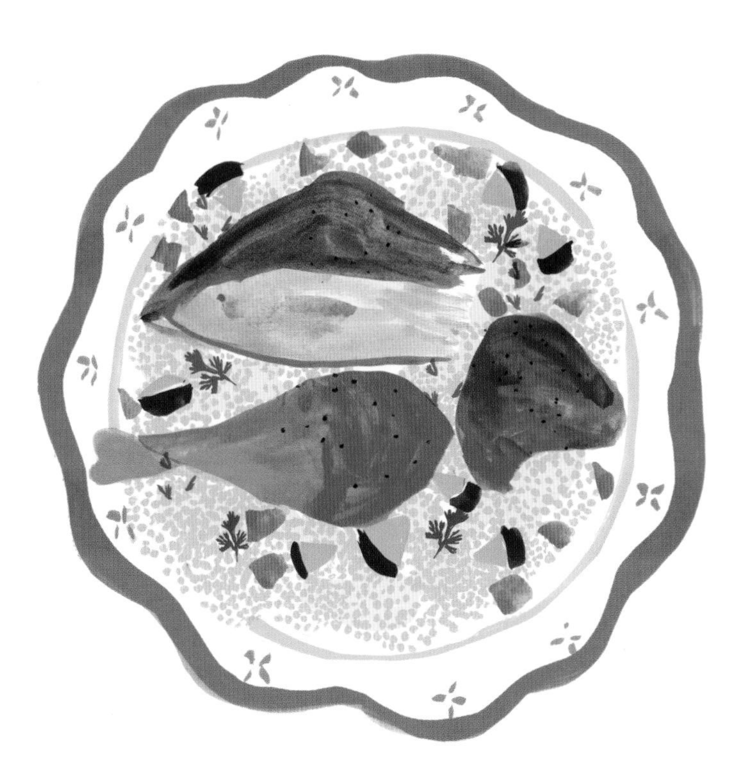

Coronation Chicken in Lettuce Cups

Our modern take on chicken salad includes chopped fresh mango and toasted coconut flakes, elegantly presented in lettuce cups for posh picnic noshing. You can poach the chicken, but we like to use a purchased rotisserie chicken from the market or leftovers from a Sunday supper.

SERVES 4 TO 6

- ⅓ cup Greek-style yogurt
- ⅓ cup D.I.Y. Mayonnaise (page 35) or store-bought mayonnaise
- ¼ cup finely chopped fresh cilantro
- 2 green onions, white and green parts only, thinly sliced
- 2 to 3 teaspoons curry powder
- ¼ teaspoon fine sea salt
- 3 cups shredded or coarsely chopped cooked chicken, chilled or at room temperature
- 1 mango, peeled, pitted, and cubed
- 1 large celery rib, thinly sliced
- ⅓ cup roasted cashews, coarsely chopped
- 1 head of butter lettuce
- ½ cup unsweetened flaked coconut, toasted (see Tiny Tip)

1. Whisk together the yogurt, mayonnaise, cilantro, green onions, 2 teaspoons of the curry powder, and the salt in a large bowl. Add the chicken, mango, celery, and cashews and stir it all together. Taste and adjust the seasoning, adding more curry powder or salt, if desired. (The salad can be made up to 1 day ahead.)

2. Trim the core from the head of lettuce and separate the leaves. Reserve the large, soft outer leaves for another use. Wash the crisper, cup-shaped interior leaves and blot dry in a kitchen towel. Fill each leaf cup with a spoonful of the chicken salad and top with coconut flakes; this can be done in advance or at the picnic site.

TINY TIP: Flaked coconut is sometimes labeled "coconut chips." You can buy it pre-toasted, or spread it in an even layer on a baking sheet and toast in a 350°F oven until lightly browned.

IN THE BASKET:

- ☐ **Butter lettuce leaves**
- ☐ **Coconut flakes**
- ☐ **Spoon**

Open Your Own Outdoor Cinema

Here's everything you need to know about setting up your own flick fest.

1. Announce the film in advance, and theme the menu around it.
2. Invite friends to tote chairs, blankets, pillows, and sleeping bags to create a cozy outdoor ambience.
3. String globe lights in the trees to construct cinema-friendly low lighting while your techie friend hooks up the projector.
4. Set up a candy bar: stack cellophane bags next to various-size containers of bulk candy and place a wooden scoop in each jar.
5. Pop popcorn as instructed on page 41 and scoop it into individual paper bags.
6. Begin the evening with a quick round of "trailers"—movie-themed charades.
7. Follow the first film with a late-night double feature; that's when the magic happens.

CHAPTER 5

Sweets

You can finally see the bottom of your basket, the sun is dipping low in the sky, a bottle of limoncello is making the rounds, and, quite naturally, a picnic's conversation drifts to sweet endings. After all, every beautiful dinner deserves an equally enticing epilogue, and as much as you love savory, nobody can blame you for being ever so slightly impatient to get to the sweet stuff. (We've even, on occasion, hosted picnics composed entirely of desserts. Highly recommend.)

Ten Fabulous Floats

Be it nostalgia or the mad-scientist appeal of ice cream coupled with a fizzy soda, everyone flips for a float. Each of these floats follows a simple three-element formula: ice cream, liquid, and garnish. But this is only the beginning; have a ball mixing and matching, experimenting with everything from cold-brew coffee to artisan sodas to bourbon.

Strawberry Ice Cream +
Strawberry Soda + Sliced Fresh Strawberries

Chocolate Ice Cream +
Cherry Soda + Muddled Bing Cherries + Bourbon

Coffee Ice Cream +
Root Beer + Chantilly Whipped Cream (page 149) + Root Beer Hard Candy Stick

Peach Ice Cream +
Ginger Beer + Muddled Peaches + Mint Sprig

Pistachio Ice Cream +
Pomegranate Soda (see Homemade Grenadine on page 163) + Mint Sprig

Neapolitan Ice Cream +
Cream Soda + Chocolate Sauce + Chopped Bananas + Amarena Cherry on Top

Salted Caramel Ice Cream +
Sparkling or Hard Apple Cider + Chopped Cinnamon-Roasted Apples

Lemon Sorbet +
Sparkling Raspberry Lemonade + Fresh Raspberries

Coconut Ice Cream +
Pineapple Soda + Pineapple Wedge + Rum

Vanilla Bean Ice Cream +
Cold Brewed Coffee + Almond Biscotti + Chocolate Shavings

Dry Ice, Demystified

When it comes to bringing ice cream or ice pops to your picnic, dry ice's arctic abilities are miraculous and will keep your frozen treats intact for hours. Here are a few tips for stress-free handling.

1. Bring your cooler to the grocery store and ask the staff for help.
2. To keep food or drinks chilly, place dry ice in the bottom of the cooler, spread a bag of regular ice on top of it, and place your items on top. Do not let the drinks touch the dry ice directly, or they will freeze.
3. To keep food (such as ice cream) frozen for up to twenty-four hours, pack it in a food-safe container and place the dry ice on top of it.
4. Remove your frozen items from the cooler five minutes before you want to serve or scoop to soften them a bit.
5. Leave the cooler open as you're eating your cold sweets, and the solid dry ice will turn back into gas and drift away, making for the easiest cleanup ever.

Tips & Tricks: Alfresco Floats

Set up an outdoor soda fountain in six easy steps.

1. Rinse six 1-pint lidded glass jars in water and place them in the freezer until frosty, at least 30 minutes.
2. Meanwhile, purchase a 5-pound brick of dry ice. In most cities, it's available at large grocery stores, but call to check before you head out. Wrap it in a kitchen towel. (See Dry Ice, Demystified, page 129.)
3. Scoop ice cream into each frosted jar—a single scoop will do the trick, but why not make it a double? Top with lids and immediately put the jars into a portable cooler. Place the dry ice on top, and they will stay frozen for up to 24 hours.
4. To pack everything in the same cooler, insert a cardboard divider to differentiate the dry ice/ice cream jar zone and the soda/garnish zone, which will be at the perfect refrigerator temperature. WARNING: Do *not* put dry ice on top of your soda. It will freeze, explode, and generally undermine your Mr. Wizard prowess.
5. At the picnic, pull the jars out of the cooler, pour in your liquid pairing of choice, garnish the floats with the proverbial cherry on top, and pop in snazzy paper straws.
6. Revive your overexcited audience with smelling salts.

Menu: La Dolce Vita

Hop on your Vespa and scoot over to a decadent partito of Italian film and food.

Five Fresh-Fruit Paletas

These fruit-forward ice pops are sunshine on a stick. Each of the following recipes makes eight paletas—for most of them, just purée the fresh fruit and sweetener in a blender on high speed until very smooth, then pour the mixture into an ice-pop mold. Use your fingers, a fork, or best yet, a chopstick to maneuver slivers of fruit or herbs into the pops, and freeze the paletas immediately, as they have a tendency to separate if left on the counter. Place the paletas in your freezer for three to four hours to completely solidify them, then take them to the picnic in a cooler outfitted with dry ice (see page 129) or keep them in the freezer for up to 1 month.

TINY TIP

Purchase an ice-pop tray (see Picnic Provisions, page 185) for universally perfect paletas, or improvise with paper cones, Dixie cups, tall shot glasses, or jelly jars. Freeze the paletas for 30 minutes and then pop a stick through the frozen surface and continue freezing. To free your paletas, peel away paper containers or take glass containers out of the cooler for a few minutes to let the hot air loosen the edges, then hold the ice-pop stick and invert.

Strawberry-Rosemary

4 cups chopped strawberries plus 2 strawberries, thinly sliced

3 tablespoons honey

1 teaspoon minced fresh rosemary

Purée the chopped strawberries, honey, and rosemary, and pour the mixture into the molds. Position 2 thin slices of fresh strawberry in the center of each pop, one on either side, and freeze.

Sugar Plum

4 cups chopped plums (about 4)

2 tablespoons sugar, or more to taste

Purée the plums and sugar, pour the mixture into molds, and freeze.

Pineapple Mint

4 cups chopped pineapple

½ cup loosely packed fresh mint leaves, plus 16 small leaves for garnish

Purée the pineapple and ½ cup mint and pour the mixture into molds. Use a chopstick to position 2 mint leaves in each pop. Freeze.

Double Grape

1 large bunch of Concord grapes, washed and halved lengthwise

2 cups Muscadet grapes, blended

1 tablespoon sugar

Distribute the halved grapes evenly among all eight molds. For the prettiest presentation, use a chopstick to place them so the cut side faces the mold. Mix the grape juice and sugar, then pour it over the grapes and freeze.

Coco-Kiwi-Mango Tango

COCO-KIWI LAYER

4 kiwis, peeled

½ cup canned coconut milk

1 tablespoon sugar

MANGO LAYER

2 cups chopped mango

2 tablespoons sugar

¼ cup canned coconut milk

1. For the kiwi layer, slice the kiwis into ½-inch rounds, then cut each one into 6 tiny triangles. Whisk the coconut milk and sugar together, fold in the kiwi triangles, and pour the mixture into the molds to fill them halfway. Freeze for 30 minutes.

2. For the mango layer, purée the mango, sugar, and coconut milk. Spoon this mixture over the partially frozen first layer to create a double-layered treat. Freeze completely.

Chocolate-Dipped Green Tea Shortbread

Adding matcha—Japanese powdered green tea—to this delicate cookie dough imparts a delightful grassy hue, while the rice flour gives the shortbread just the right tender bite. Partially dipped in melted chocolate and sprinkled with flecks of pistachio, these make a chic ending to an outdoor meal.

MAKES 50 COOKIES

½ pound (2 sticks) unsalted butter, cubed, at room temperature

½ cup sugar

1½ cups all-purpose flour

½ cup rice flour

¼ teaspoon fine sea salt

1 tablespoon matcha (see Tiny Tips)

6 ounces bittersweet chocolate chips

¼ cup shelled and peeled pistachios, finely chopped

IN THE BASKET:

- ☐ **Cookie platter or tall Mason jars for serving**

1. Cream the butter and sugar in the bowl of a stand mixer with a paddle attachment, or in a large bowl with an electric mixer, on medium-high speed until pale yellow. Mix together the flours, salt, and matcha in a separate bowl. Gradually add the dry ingredients to the butter and sugar and mix on low speed, or by hand, until the dough starts to pull away from the sides of the bowl.

2. Dump the dough onto the center of a sheet of parchment paper (or plastic wrap). Using the parchment paper, pat and roll the dough into a cylinder about 1½ inches in diameter. Roll it up tightly in the paper and twist the ends closed. Refrigerate the dough until firm, at least 1 hour and up to 2 days before baking, or wrap tightly in plastic and freeze for up to 1 month.

3. Position racks in the upper and lower thirds of the oven and preheat it to 200°F. Line two cookie sheets with parchment paper.

4. Unwrap the dough and cut it into ¼-inch rounds. Place the rounds on the prepared cookie sheets at least 1 inch apart and bake until the bottoms look dry and the cookies are slightly crisp, rotating the pans

halfway through, 50 to 55 minutes. Cool to room temperature.

5. Gently melt the chocolate chips in a double boiler or in 30-second increments in a microwave, whisking occasionally, until the chocolate is shiny and smooth.

6. Dip the cooled cookies about a third of the way into the melted chocolate, then sprinkle each with a generous pinch of pistachios over the wet chocolate. Return the cookies to the parchment paper to cool and harden. Once cooled, layer them between sheets of parchment paper in a portable container. The cookies will keep for up to 5 days.

TINY TIPS:

Find matcha online or at your favorite teahouse, upscale grocer, Asian market, or specialty shop.

These colorful cookies make a perfect party favor. Stack eight cookies in a tall 8-ounce Mason jar, alternating the direction of the chocolate for a yin-yang effect. Write the recipe or a sweet note on a tag and attach it to the jar with jute twine or decorative ribbon.

Lemon Lavender Cream Pots

Besides being the cutest thing since Bernese mountain dog puppies, these jars of buttery lemon curd are the ideal size for a single dessert portion, and they travel like a pro. When you arrive, top the lemon pots with freshly whipped lavender-infused cream and a flower petal.

MAKES 6

- 3 large eggs, at room temperature
- 3 large egg yolks, at room temperature
- ⅔ cup plus ½ teaspoon sugar
- 1½ tablespoons grated lemon zest (about 2 large lemons)
- ½ cup plus 2 tablespoons fresh lemon juice (about 3 large lemons)
- 4 tablespoons (½ stick) unsalted butter, cubed
- 3 fresh lavender buds or ¼ teaspoon dried lavender
- ⅓ cup heavy cream
- 6 small rose petals or other edible flowers (optional)

IN THE BASKET:

- ☐ **Whipped cream**
- ☐ **Quenelle spoons**
- ☐ **Edible flowers**

1. Fill a medium saucepan with about 2 inches of water and bring it to a simmer over medium heat.

2. Whisk together the eggs, egg yolks, the ⅔ cup sugar, and the lemon zest in a large metal bowl. Whisk in the lemon juice. Place the bowl over the simmering water and cook, whisking constantly but slowly, until the mixture thickens to the consistency of sour cream, about 10 minutes.

3. Remove the pan from the heat and whisk in the butter until melted. Strain the lemon curd through a fine-mesh strainer into a large bowl. Ladle it into 4-ounce glass canning jars with lids, distributing evenly and leaving at least ½ inch headspace. Tap each jar gently on the counter to distribute the curd evenly and smooth the tops. Wipe the rims clean, seal the jars, and refrigerate until the lemon curd is thickened and completely cold, about 4 hours. The lemon pots can be made up to 3 days before the picnic.

4. Meanwhile, add the lavender to the cream and refrigerate for 1 to 2 hours to infuse. Strain and discard the lavender and refrigerate the cream until needed.

5. Just before leaving for the picnic, pour the cold lavender-infused cream and the remaining ½ teaspoon of sugar in a large metal bowl and whisk briskly until soft peaks form (when the whisk is drawn from the cream, a peak forms and curls over). Put the softly whipped cream into a sealable container to transport to the picnic.

6. To serve, use two small spoons to make oval-shaped dollops (quenelles) of whipped cream and place one atop each lemon pot. Garnish with the petals, if using.

TINY TIP:
Leftover curd? Spoon it over scones, pound cake, warm biscuits, or pancakes, roll it into crepes, or fold it into Chantilly Whipped Cream (page 149) for an easy lemon mousse.

Vanilla Bean Shortcakes
with Strawberries in Basil Syrup

Strawberry shortcake gets an update when berries swim in an herbaceous simple syrup. If you're short on time, this quick topping is also delicious on a store-bought angel food cake.

MAKES 8

Topping

1½ pounds strawberries, sliced (about 2 pints)

2 tablespoon tiny fresh basil leaves, or thinly sliced large basil leaves

1 batch Basil Simple Syrup (page 169)

Shortcakes

2 cups all-purpose flour

1 tablespoon granulated sugar

1 tablespoon baking powder

¾ teaspoon baking soda

½ teaspoon fine sea salt

8 tablespoons (1 stick) unsalted butter, cubed and chilled in the freezer for at least 10 minutes

1 vanilla bean, halved lengthwise

¾ cup buttermilk

1 large egg

1 tablespoon water

Turbinado or granulated sugar, for sprinkling

Chantilly Whipped Cream (page 149)

1. To make the topping: Fill a 1-quart jar with the strawberries and basil and pour the syrup over them. Replace the lid and invert the jar a few times, so that the syrup coats the berries and basil. Let the topping stand for at least 30 minutes, or up to 1 day in the refrigerator. Invert the jar occasionally.

2. To make the shortcakes: Preheat the oven to 425°F.

3. Sift the flour, granulated sugar, baking powder, baking soda, and salt together into a large bowl. Add the butter and combine using a pastry cutter or your fingertips until the butter is broken into pea-size bits.

4. Scrape the seeds from the vanilla bean into the buttermilk and stir to distribute. Stir the buttermilk into the dry ingredients with a rubber spatula just until the dough comes together. Dump the dough onto a well-floured countertop and pat it into a 1½-inch-thick disk. Cut the disk into 8 wedges and place them on a cookie sheet at least 2 inches apart. Whisk the egg and water together until foamy. Brush the shortcakes lightly with the egg wash and sprinkle them with turbinado sugar.

5. Bake until the tops are golden and the bottoms toasty, 14 to 16 minutes.

6. Cool, then wrap the shortcakes in an attractive kitchen towel and put in the basket along with the toppings. At the picnic, slice the shortcakes in half and spoon strawberries and syrup over the bottoms. Top with dollops of whipped cream and cap with the remaining halves of the shortcakes.

IN THE BASKET:

- ☐ Topping
- ☐ Serving spoon
- ☐ Knife
- ☐ Whipping cream + whisk + metal bowl (if whipping on-site)

Hazelnut Orange Picnic Cakes

Even though these darling little cakes are exceptionally tender and decadent, they're still sturdy enough to pack and go, making them a cinch to bring to a picnic, especially if you tote them in their muffin tin.

MAKES 12

1 cup unsalted hazelnuts
½ pound (2 sticks) unsalted butter
1 teaspoon pure vanilla extract
2 tablespoons orange liqueur, such as Grand Marnier
1 cup powdered sugar
½ cup all-purpose flour
¼ teaspoon fine sea salt
1 tablespoon grated orange zest (from the 2 large oranges)
6 large egg whites
2 large oranges

IN THE BASKET:

- ☐ **Jar of orange wedges in syrup**
- ☐ **Platter**
- ☐ **Spoon**

1. Preheat the oven to 350°F. Roast the hazelnuts on a baking sheet until toasted and crackly, about 15 minutes. (Watch closely; they'll burn if neglected.) Take the roasted nuts out of the oven and wrap them in a slightly damp kitchen towel. Cool for 5 minutes, then rub them vigorously with the towel to remove as much of the skins as possible. Cool the hazelnuts to room temperature.

2. Meanwhile, melt the butter in a small saucepan, turn off the heat, add the vanilla and 1 tablespoon of the orange liqueur, and set aside to cool slightly.

3. Grind the hazelnuts to a fine meal in a food processor. Add the powdered sugar and pulse a few times to blend, then pulse in the flour and salt and, finally, the orange zest; set aside.

4. Whip the egg whites in a stand mixer with the whisk attachment until they hold stiff peaks. Alternately fold the hazelnut mixture and the butter mixture into the egg whites one-third at a time, starting with the dry ingredients. Wipe out the butter saucepan with a paper towel and use that to grease a 12-cup muffin tin.

5. Distribute the batter evenly among the muffin cups and bake until the cakes are golden and spring back

when pressed lightly in the center, 20 to 25 minutes. Cool for 15 minutes in the pan, then run a knife gently around each one and pop them out. Finish cooling them on a wire rack.

6. Trim the pith off the zested oranges with a sharp knife, then segment the oranges by cutting between the membranes, reserving the wedges and juice in a 1-pint Mason jar. Stir in the remaining tablespoon of orange liqueur and refrigerate until you leave for the picnic.

7. At the picnic, invert the cakes onto a platter, and spoon orange wedges and a teaspoon or two of syrup over each one. These cakes keep for 3 or 4 days in a tightly sealed container, and can be frozen for up to a month and thawed the day of the picnic.

TINY TIP: If making these during tangerine season, try substituting a half-dozen tangerines for the oranges, and serve a bowl of leaf- and stem-clad tangerines alongside for an au naturel accompaniment.

If you have a stovetop within easy reach—who doesn't love a porch picnic?—pour warm ganache over the top of each cake for extra chocolate oomph before adorning them with the oranges.

Sugar Rush

Sometimes the best desserts are the simplest, and nobody is going to kick you off the blanket for bringing chocolate.

If a homemade dessert doesn't fit into your packed schedule, choose from a myriad of sweet treats that are grab and go—bring a colorful assortment of macarons or petits fours, a jar of soft caramels, a fun bag of nostalgic confections from your favorite candy shop, or a mashup of good-quality chocolate bars, barks, and bonbons.

Chocolate has trouble keeping its composure in high heat, so Portland chocolatiers (and fellow picnickers) Sarah Hart and Hannah Sullivan of Alma Chocolate recommend transporting it wrapped in a plastic bag inside a cooler, then removing it immediately before serving. Should melting occur, don't sweat it—bring backup bread, graham crackers, fruit, or pretzels and improvise a delicious dip. Or use the heat to your advantage by bringing chunks of dark chocolate tucked into a crusty baguette, and let it sit out for a few minutes to create a warm, oozy pain au chocolat on the fly.

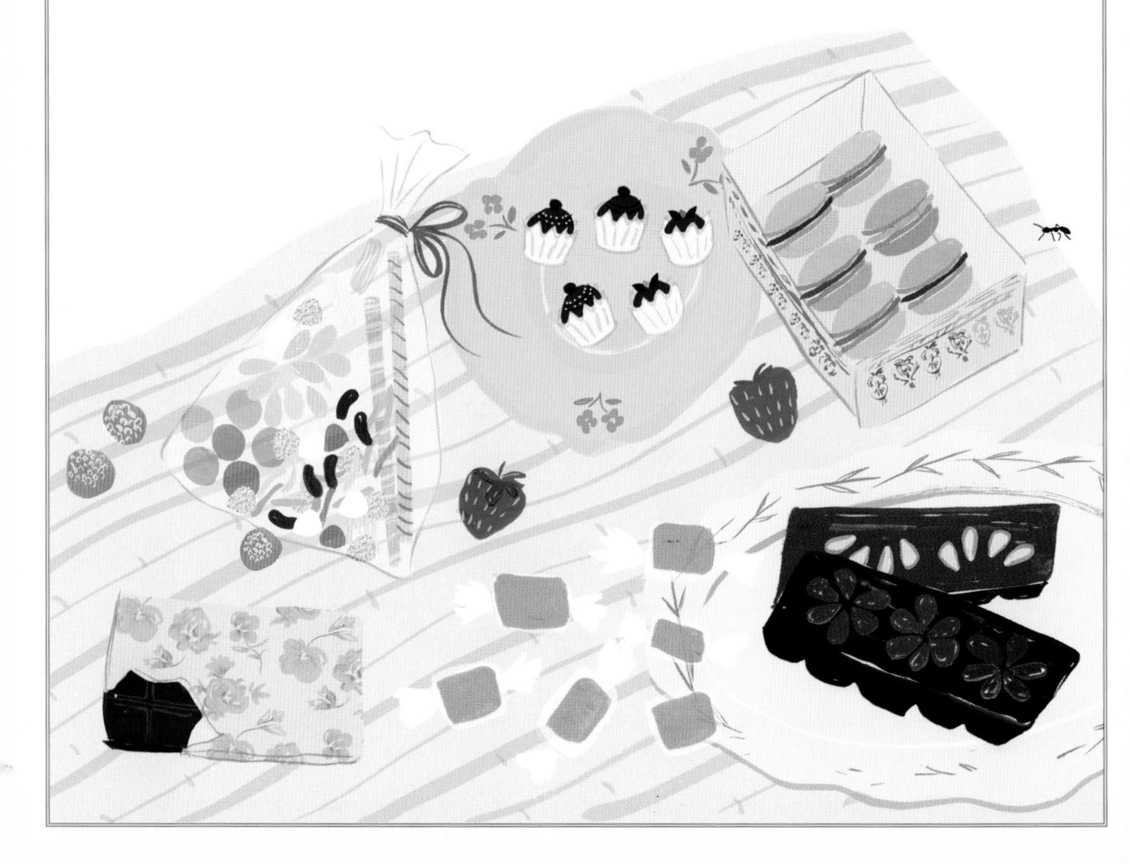

Spicy Salted Olive Oil Brownies

The beloved brownie gets a Mediterranean makeover with ground espresso, a hit of spice, and lots of olive oil, conjuring a thick, luscious, rich, and fudgy treat that gets better with time.

MAKES 25 BROWNIES

- ⅔ cup mild olive oil, plus more for greasing the pan
- ½ cup all-purpose flour
- 1 cup unsweetened cocoa powder
- 1 tablespoon finely ground espresso beans or instant espresso
- ½ teaspoon fine sea salt
- ¼ teaspoon cayenne
- 2 large eggs
- 2 large egg yolks
- 1¼ cups granulated sugar
- 1 teaspoon pure vanilla extract
- Coarse sea salt, such as fleur de sel or Maldon, for sprinkling

1. Preheat the oven to 325°F. Line an 8-by-8-inch baking pan with foil and grease it with oil. Mix together the flour, cocoa powder, espresso, salt, and cayenne in a large bowl. In another large bowl, whisk together the eggs, yolks, sugar, and vanilla until smooth, then slowly pour in the olive oil, whisking to emulsify.

2. Pour half of the dry ingredients into the wet ingredients and mix to incorporate, then add the remaining dry ingredients and mix well. Spread the batter evenly into the prepared baking pan. Bake until the top appears dry and the center is still moist but firm, 30 to 35 minutes. Remove from the oven and immediately sprinkle with the coarse salt.

3. Cool, then cut the brownies into 1½-inch squares (5 rows by 5 rows) and arrange them on a platter. Cover tightly for transport. The brownies will keep for up to 4 days.

Petite Pavlovas
with Limey Roasted Rhubarb

We count pastry chef Kristen Murray of Maurice, in Portland, as one of our picnicking own. We love her pillowy pavlovas best with heaps of our velvety Chantilly Whipped Cream (page 149) and tangy Greek yogurt, bedecked by cubes of bright pink roasted rhubarb in its own lime zest–flecked syrup.

MAKES 12

Limey Roasted Rhubarb

2 pounds rhubarb, trimmed and cut into ½-inch cubes (for most stalks, that means slicing lengthwise in thirds, and then horizontally)

⅔ cup packed dark brown sugar

2 teaspoons grated lime zest

2 tablespoons fresh lime juice

Pavlova

7 large egg whites, at room temperature

Pinch sea salt

1½ cups sugar

2 teaspoons Champagne or white wine vinegar

1 tablespoon plus 1 teaspoon cornstarch

Whipped Topping

½ cup full- or low-fat Greek-style yogurt

1 batch Chantilly Whipped Cream (page 149)

IN THE BASKET:

- ☐ **Pavlovas**
- ☐ **Container of whipped topping**
- ☐ **Roasted rhubarb in syrup**
- ☐ **Spoons**

1. To roast the rhubarb: Preheat the oven to 350°F. Line a large rimmed baking sheet with aluminum foil.

2. Toss together the rhubarb, brown sugar, lime zest, and juice in a large bowl. Spread the mixture on the prepared baking sheet and roast until the rhubarb is very tender but still holds its shape and the juice is syrupy, 15 to 20 minutes. Cool the rhubarb and syrup to room temperature, then scrape it into a container with a tight-fitting lid and refrigerate until the picnic.

3. To make the pavlovas: Reduce the oven temperature to 300°F. Line two cookie sheets with parchment paper.

4. Beat the egg whites on medium-high speed in a stand mixer fitted with a whisk attachment, or in a large bowl with an electric mixer, until foamy, about one minute. Add the salt, then add the sugar in a small stream until completely incorporated. Continue whipping until the meringue is shiny and glossier than 1980s hair mousse, about 3 minutes.

5. Drizzle in the vinegar and then sift the cornstarch over the meringue, and gently fold both in without deflating the mixture.

6. Spoon the meringue into a pastry bag or gallon-size resealable plastic bag with the corner snipped off, and pipe it into twelve 4-inch-wide mounds on the prepared sheets. Using the back of a spoon, create a shallow well in the center of each.

7. Place both sheets in the oven and immediately reduce the temperature to 225°F. Bake for 30 minutes. Turn the oven off and cool the pavlovas completely, with the oven door closed, at least 2 hours or overnight. Pack the pavlovas in an airtight plastic container, gently stacking them in two layers with parchment paper in between. These are best served within 1 day of baking, but undressed pavlovas will keep for up to 2 days in an airtight container.

8. To make the whipped topping: Gently fold the yogurt into the whipped cream in a large bowl. Pack the topping into a container with a tight-fitting lid to transport to the picnic.

9. Once at the picnic, spoon some of the whipped topping into the well of each pavlova, then top with the roasted rhubarb and syrup and serve.

TINY TIP:
If your eggs aren't room temperature, put them in a bowl of warm water for 10 minutes.

Banana à Trois Pudding Parfaits

If you like bananas even a little bit, chances are you'll like this dessert a lot. Our parfait is a veritable banana bomb, with mashed bananas mixed into the bread, roasted bananas folded into the pudding, and fresh bananas placed on top.

SERVES 8

Praline Crumble

1 large egg white

⅓ cup packed dark brown sugar

½ teaspoon pure vanilla extract

⅛ teaspoon salt

1 cup pecan halves

Banana Bread

8 tablespoons (1 stick) unsalted butter

1½ cups all-purpose flour, plus more for dusting

1 teaspoon baking soda

¼ teaspoon fine sea salt

1 cup granulated sugar

2 large eggs

1 teaspoon pure vanilla extract

2 overripe bananas, mashed

½ cup sour cream

Pudding

⅓ cup granulated sugar

3 tablespoons cornstarch

¼ teaspoon fine sea salt

2¼ cups whole milk

3 large egg yolks

3 tablespoons unsalted butter, cubed

1 tablespoon spiced rum or bourbon

1 teaspoon pure vanilla extract

2 underripe bananas, roasted and mashed (see Tiny Tip) or 2 overripe bananas

1½ cups Chantilly Whipped Cream (page 149)

1 perfect banana, peeled and diced

1. To make the crumble: Preheat the oven to 300°F and line a cookie sheet with parchment paper. Whisk the egg white in a bowl until frothy. Add the brown sugar, vanilla, and salt, and whisk to combine. Pour the pecans into the mixture and stir to coat them evenly. Spread the mixture in a single layer on the cookie sheet and bake, stirring occasionally, until nicely browned, about 25 minutes. Set aside to cool, then roughly chop.

2. To make the banana bread: Preheat the oven to 350°F and grease and flour a standard loaf pan. Sift the flour, baking soda, and salt together and set aside. Cream the butter and sugar in an electric mixer on medium-high speed, then add the eggs one at a time. Reduce the speed to low and add the vanilla, overripe bananas, and sour cream. Bake until cooked through, 1 to 1¼ hours. (A toothpick will come out clean.) Cool on a baking rack. Once cool, invert the bread onto a cutting board, cut it into ½-inch slices, and punch out eight 2½-inch circles of bread with a biscuit cutter.

3. To make the pudding: Whisk together the sugar, cornstarch, and salt in a medium saucepan. Pour in ¼ cup of the milk and whisk until smooth with no visible lumps. Whisk in the egg yolks and then the remaining 2 cups milk.

4. Place over medium heat and cook, whisking often, until the pudding is slightly thickened, 5 to 6 minutes. Reduce the heat to medium-low and switch to a silicone spatula. Cook, stirring constantly, scraping the bottom and sides of the pan, until the pudding is thickened and sticks to the spatula.

5. Remove the pan from the heat, add the butter, liquor, and vanilla, and stir until the butter is completely melted. (If the pudding has small lumps, try whisking briskly to work them out.) Transfer the pudding to the bowl of a food processor and blend the roasted bananas into the mixture. Transfer to a large measuring cup, or another container with a spout, and cool to room temperature. Cover the surface of the pudding with plastic wrap to keep a skin from forming.

6. Build the parfaits in six 8-ounce, clear-glass jelly jars (see illustration). Begin with a spoonful of room-temperature pudding. Don't worry if the pudding is a little thin—it will thicken up when it sets in the refrigerator. Layer with pralines and more pudding. Press a bread round into each jar. Add another layer of pudding, a sprinkle of diced bananas, and a spoonful of Chantilly Whipped Cream to reach the top of the jar. Cover the jars with lids and refrigerate for at least 1 hour, or for up to 1 day before the picnic.

TINY TIP: If you're in need of overripe bananas and none are in sight, bake ripe bananas whole in a 300°F oven for 30 minutes, until the peels are entirely black and the fruit is soft, sweet, and inimitably banana-y. Peel and use.

Parfait Primer

For the best bite imaginable, build parfaits in this order.

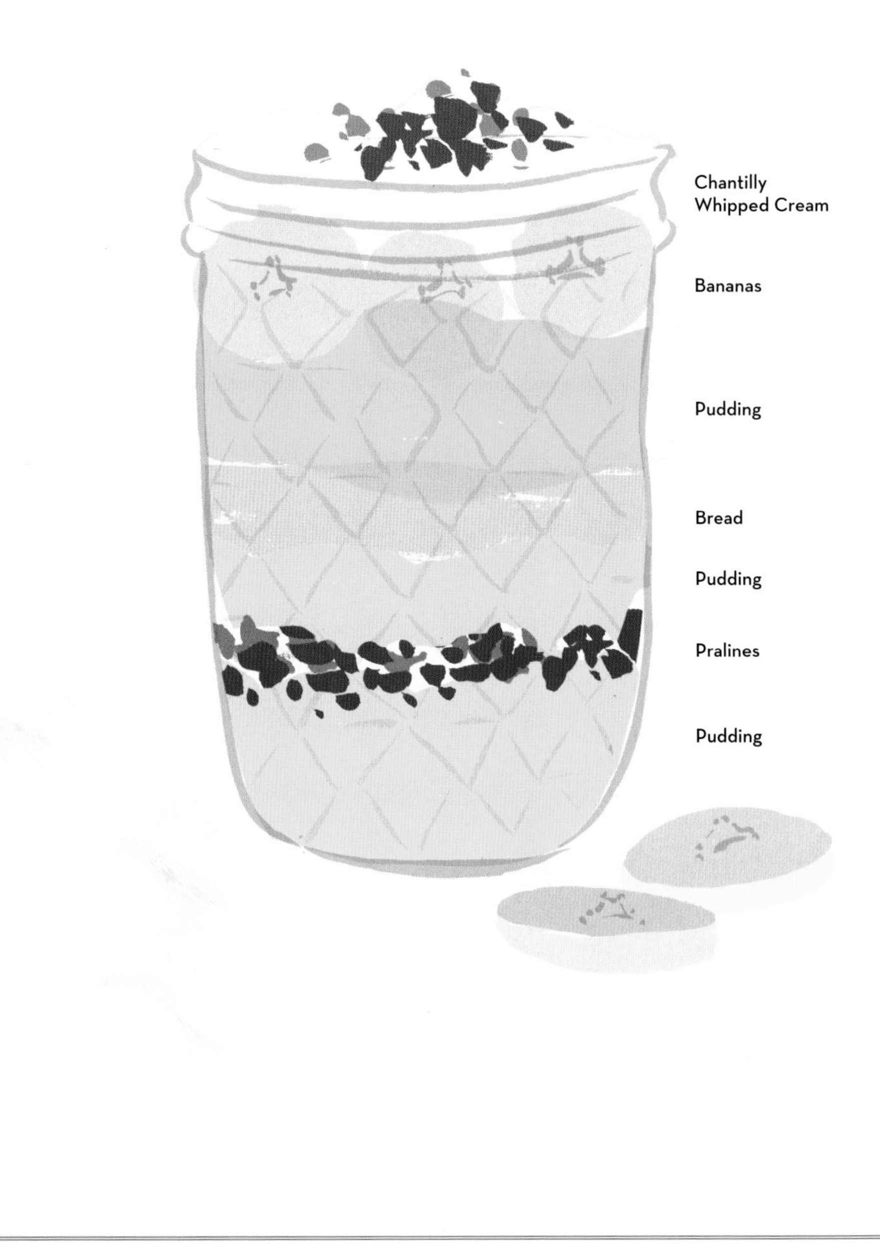

Chantilly Whipped Cream

Chantilly cream—softly whipped cream sweetened with sugar and flavored with vanilla—is a decadent addition to so many picnic desserts. Making it is easy as can be, and the homemade version is so much better than the store-bought kind. Just be sure to avoid over-whipping; the goal is silky-smooth fluff, not stiff foam. If you're a perfectionist with a wrist of steel, bring a whisk and a mixing bowl to whip the cream on-site, or for an effortless shortcut, purchase a reusable whipped cream dispenser, put the ingredients inside, and let the gadget do the whipping for you.

MAKES ABOUT 2 CUPS

1 cup very cold heavy (whipping) cream
1 tablespoon sugar
¼ teaspoon pure vanilla extract

Place the cream, sugar, and vanilla in a stand mixer fitted with the whisk attachment and whip on medium speed until soft peaks form (when the whisk is drawn from the cream, a peak forms and curls over). Alternatively, whip the cream in a large metal bowl using a whisk or a handheld electric mixer. Cover and refrigerate until the picnic, or for up to 1 day, then transport in a cooler.

Stone Fruit Galette

The amount of sugar you'll need for this free-form tart depends wholly on the sweetness or tartness of the fruit, and your taste, of course. Thoroughly sample your fruits before assembling the galette, and add a few more tablespoons of sugar if they are particularly puckery.

SERVES 8

- 1 batch Perfect Pie Dough (page 107)
- 2 tablespoons all-purpose flour, plus more for rolling the dough
- ½ cup slivered almonds
- ½ cup packed light brown sugar
- 1 pound ripe peaches or nectarines, halved, pitted, and cut into ½-inch wedges
- 1 pound ripe plums, halved, pitted, and cut into ½-inch wedges
- 2 tablespoons unsalted butter, cubed
- Heavy cream
- 1 tablespoon turbinado sugar (optional)

IN THE BASKET:

- ☐ **Knife**
- ☐ **Pastry server**

1. Preheat the oven to 400°F. Line a large rimmed baking sheet with parchment paper.

2. Roll out the pie dough to a 13-inch circle on a lightly floured countertop using a floured rolling pin. The dough will be moist, so rotate it occasionally to be sure it isn't sticking, and dust with additional flour as needed. Roll the dough up loosely onto the rolling pin and unroll it onto the lined baking sheet. Loosely fold in any overhanging edges and refrigerate until cold and firm, about 20 minutes.

3. Put the almonds and ¼ cup of the brown sugar in the food processor and process to a fine meal. Add the 2 tablespoons flour and process until well mixed.

4. Spread the almond meal over the rolled-out dough, leaving a 2-inch border. Arrange the peaches and plums over the almond meal in an even layer. Sprinkle the fruit with the remaining ¼ cup brown sugar and dot the top with butter. Fold the edges over the filling, overlapping as needed to create an evenly pleated crust. Brush the crust lightly with cream and sprinkle with turbinado sugar, if using.

5. Bake the galette until the edges are nicely browned and crisp and the fruit is soft and bubbly, about 1 hour. Excess juices will ooze onto the pan and harden as the galette bakes, so slide a knife under the crust to free it after cooling. Cool completely before wrapping the galette loosely with plastic, and transport it to the picnic on the baking sheet or a round platter. Slice and serve at the picnic site. Wrap any leftover galette slices and snack on them for up to 3 days.

Apricot Almond Franny

Thrilled to be made a day ahead, sturdy enough to tote in a basket, and impervious to temperature changes, Mademoiselle Franny is unflappable. And with apricots nestled in nutty browned butter and a cookie crust, she's as tasty as it gets.

SERVES 8

Tart Shell

½ cup almond flour (see Tiny Tips)
¾ cup all-purpose flour
Pinch of fine sea salt
¼ cup granulated sugar
7 tablespoons unsalted butter, melted

Filling

8 tablespoons (1 stick) unsalted butter
¼ cup (2½ ounces) almond paste, packed
⅓ cup sugar
1 vanilla bean, split and seeds scraped (see Tiny Tips)
2 large eggs
¼ cup all-purpose flour
Pinch of fine sea salt
3 ripe apricots

Topping

½ cup sliced blanched almonds
1 tablespoon unsalted butter, melted
1 tablespoon sugar

IN THE BASKET:

- ☐ **Large plate**
- ☐ **Sharp knife**

1. To make the tart shell: Position a rack in the center of the oven and preheat it to 375°F.
2. Whisk together the flours and salt in a medium bowl; set aside. In another bowl, stir the sugar and melted butter with a rubber spatula. Add the dry mixture to the wet mixture in ½-cup increments and stir just to combine. Dump the dough into the center of a 9-inch tart pan with a removable bottom and use a rubber spatula and your fingertips to press the crust into the bottom and up the sides of the pan in an even layer.
3. Bake on a rimmed baking sheet until golden brown, about 18 minutes. Set aside to cool to room temperature. (Leave oven on at 375°F.)
4. To make the filling: Cook the butter in a small pot over medium heat, stirring often. Watch it carefully: It will begin to turn toasty brown after about 7 minutes. In another minute, it will begin to smell like the best thing in the world and the milk solids will darken in color. That's when you pour it into a measuring cup, scraping the solids from the bottom of the pot. It should be deep brown. (If it's not, cook it for another 30 seconds. You do not want it to burn.) Set the browned butter aside to cool.

5. Meanwhile, pulse together the almond paste, sugar, and vanilla seeds in a food processor until combined. While the processor is running, add the eggs, one at a time, and process until light and fluffy. Add the browned butter, scraping in all the milk solids, then the flour and salt and process to combine. Pour the filling into the cooled tart shell.

6. Score the apricots and blanch in boiling water for 30 seconds, then transfer to an ice bath to cool. Peel, halve, and cut the apricots into ¼-inch-thick slices. Arrange the slices on top of the filling in concentric circles, with each slice overlapping slightly. Imperfection encouraged.

7. To make the topping: Combine the almonds, butter, and sugar in a small bowl. Sprinkle it evenly over the top of the tart.

8. Bake the tart on the baking sheet at 375°F until a toothpick inserted into the center comes out clean, about 40 minutes. Rotate halfway through the cooking time and tent the crust with foil if it's getting too dark. Cool on a rack.

9. Keep the cooled tart in the pan, cover it, and store at room temperature. At the picnic, remove the outer ring of the tart pan, place the tart on a plate, and slice into wedges. Leftovers will keep in the refrigerator for up to 3 days in an airtight container.

TINY TIPS:
Purchase almond flour, or simply make it yourself by grinding ½ cup almonds to a fine meal in a food processor.

Save the vanilla bean to make Vanilla-Peach Sweet Tea (page 167).

Variation

If ripe apricots are not available, substitute peaches, nectarines, apples, or raspberries.

Dueling French Picnics

Menu: Picnic in Provence

Whether you're picnicking in the Champ de Mars or lounging in a meadow of lavender in Provence (or just dreaming of either), French fare constitutes an ideal feast. Pick your pleasures.

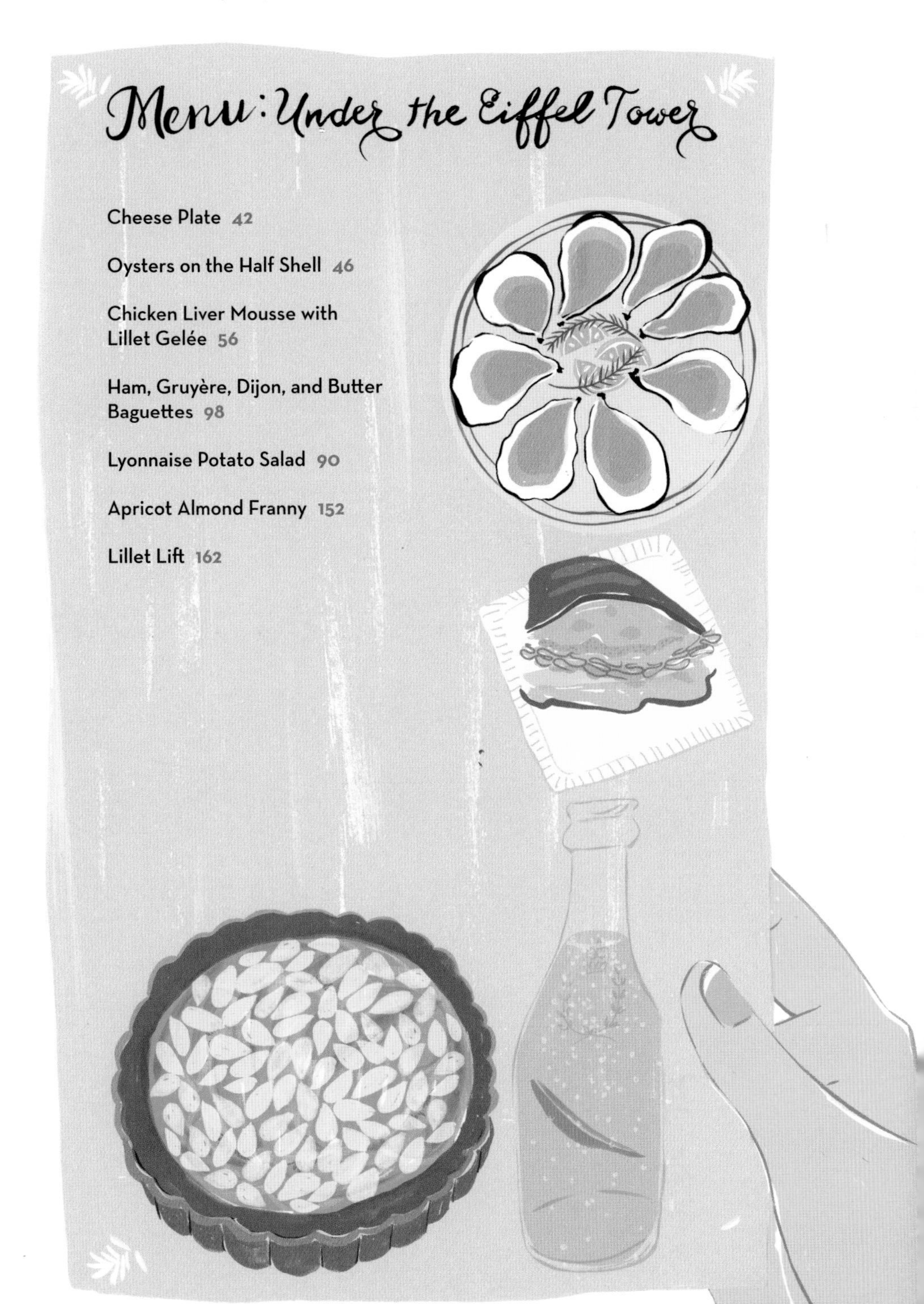

Menu: Under the Eiffel Tower

Peachy Keen Mason Jar Pies

Good things come in small jars, as evidenced by these Lilliputian peach pies baked right inside 4-ounce jelly jars. With a bit of brown sugar, a dash of bourbon, and some fancy lattice fingerwork, this Southern-summer-inspired finisher turns into quite the little looker.

MAKES 6

2 large peaches

¼ cup packed light brown sugar

⅛ teaspoon fine sea salt

1 tablespoon cornstarch

½ teaspoon pure vanilla extract

1 tablespoon bourbon

1 batch Perfect Pie Dough (page 107)

1 large egg

1 tablespoon water

Turbinado or granulated sugar, for sprinkling

IN THE BASKET:

- ☐ **Spoons**
- ☐ **Vanilla bean ice cream on dry ice (if serving ice cream)**
- ☐ **Ice cream scoop and jar lids (if serving ice cream)**

1. Score the peaches and blanch in boiling water for 30 seconds, then transfer to an ice bath to cool. Peel, pit, and cut the peaches into ½-inch dice. Place in a medium bowl and toss with the brown sugar, salt, cornstarch, vanilla, and bourbon. Refrigerate the mixture until chilled. (Make the pie dough, if you haven't already.)

2. Preheat the oven to 350°F. Line a rimmed baking sheet with parchment paper or aluminum foil.

3. Cut the chilled disk of dough into 8 equal wedges and set aside 2 for the lattice. Shape each wedge into a ball, then roll it into a 6-inch round on a lightly floured countertop; sprinkle the dough and rolling pin with flour as necessary to prevent sticking. Fold the disk into a 4-ounce Mason jar, pressing it against the sides of the jar to evenly distribute the folds of dough. Use a sharp paring knife to trim the dough hanging over the rim of the jar. Distribute the filling evenly among the jars. Once all the rounds are trimmed, gather the scraps of dough together with the remaining wedges of dough and roll them back out into a rectangle. Using a fluted pastry wheel or pizza cutter, cut out 36 strips, each measuring 3 inches

long and about ½ inch wide. Build the lattice tops. Chill the miniature pies in the freezer for 10 minutes.

4. Whisk together the egg and water in a small bowl until foamy. Lightly brush the tops of the pies with the egg wash, sprinkle them with turbinado sugar, and place them on the prepared baking sheet. Bake until the crust is golden and the filling is bubbly, 40 to 50 minutes.

5. The filling may ooze over the sides a little, so once the pies have cooled slightly, wipe the jars clean with a damp kitchen towel. Cool the pies to room temperature. For transport, wrap each jar in a cloth napkin or parchment paper tied with twine or ribbon. If desired, serve scoops of vanilla bean ice cream (packed in dry ice; see page 129) on top of each pie. Or bring the jar lids along, invert them, and serve scoops inside. Leftovers will keep for 3 days.

Blueberry Cardamom Crisps

Take your summer blueberry crop straight from the patch to the jar with darling single portions of a classic crisp.

SERVES 8

Topping

½ cup all-purpose flour

½ cup rolled oats

3 tablespoons light brown sugar

½ teaspoon ground cardamom

⅛ teaspoon fine sea salt

6 tablespoons cold unsalted butter, cubed

Filling

4 cups fresh blueberries

⅔ cup packed light brown sugar

2 tablespoons cornstarch

¼ teaspoon fine sea salt

¼ teaspoon finely grated lemon zest

1 tablespoon fresh lemon juice

1. Preheat the oven to 350°F. Line a rimmed baking sheet with aluminum foil.
2. To make the topping: In a bowl, stir together the flour, oats, brown sugar, cardamom, and salt. Add the butter and rub the mixture together with your fingertips until the butter is broken into pea-size bits. Chill in the freezer for 15 minutes while you make the filling.
3. To make the filling: In a bowl, stir together the blueberries, brown sugar, cornstarch, salt, and lemon zest and juice.
4. Divide the blueberry filling evenly among eight 4-ounce heatproof glass jars, pressing on the berries with the back of a spoon so that they are snug in the jar, and leaving about ¼-inch headspace for the topping. Spoon the topping into each jar, dividing it evenly. Place the jars on the prepared baking sheet and bake until the topping is crisp and the filling is bubbling slightly, 18 to 20 minutes.

IN THE BASKET:

- ☐ **Spoons**
- ☐ **Vanilla bean ice cream on dry ice (if serving ice cream)**
- ☐ **Ice cream scoop (if serving ice cream)**

5. The filling will ooze out a little, so once the crisps have cooled to room temperature, wipe off the jars and screw on the lids for transport. Serve scoops of vanilla bean ice cream (packed in dry ice, see page 129) on top of each crisp, or in the inverted jar lids for a little extra country-chic oomph. Recap leftovers and enjoy within three days. Or, freeze cooked or uncooked crisps for up to a month, then bake and take.

CHAPTER 6

Sips

Sips are second to none in keeping guests happy at an outdoor party, particularly when temperatures peak. Since you're bound to drink more in the summer heat, and since liquids are heavy, it's best to ask everyone to bring their own water as well as a shareable sip. (A good rule of thumb is to expect guests to sip two drinks per hour in the height of the heat.) Keep the picnickers revived and refreshed by serving a mix of nonalcoholic and alcoholic options, with an eye to the time of the party and the occasion.

Five Bubblers in a Bottle

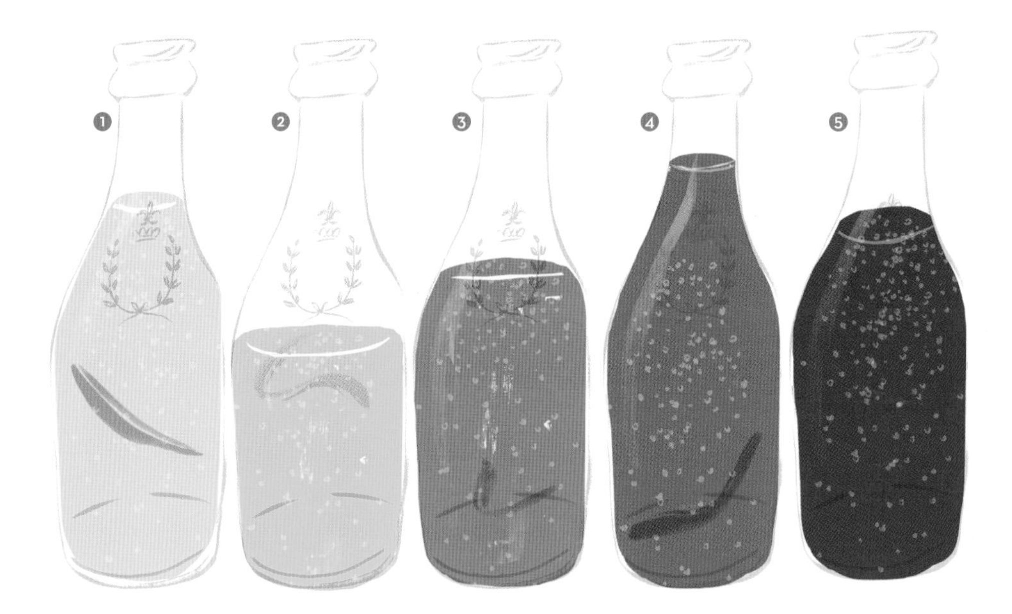

When our resident cocktail queen, Katie Burnett, brought spritzers to our picnic in tiny bottles, we were enchanted. Bottled cocktails are whimsical, portable, and—well, we'll cop to it—effective when dodging the park patrol. (Not that we'd recommend anything but completely legal alcohol consumption.) See a tutorial on how to bottle your libations in Bottled Cocktails 101 (page 164) and pack one of these five fabulous drinks (one is alcohol-free) in your cooler. Each recipe makes one drink.

1. Lillet Lift

3 ounces Lillet Blanc
2 dashes orange bitters
4 ounces Champagne
1 twist of orange zest

Using a funnel, pour the Lillet and orange bitters into a 187-ml bottle. Top with the Champagne, add the twist, and cap the bottle.

2. Americano

1½ ounces Campari
1½ ounces Cinzano Rosso vermouth
4 ounces club soda
1 twist of lemon zest

Using a funnel, pour the Campari and vermouth into a 187-ml bottle. Top with the club soda, add the twist, and cap the bottle.

3. Aperol Spritz

2 ounces Aperol
4 ounces Prosecco
1 ounce club soda
1 twist of orange zest

Using a funnel, pour the Aperol into a 187-ml bottle. Top with the Prosecco and club soda, add the twist, and cap the bottle.

4. Le Suzette

1 ounce Suze liqueur
1 ounce Lillet Blanc
1 ounce gin
4 ounces club soda
1 twist orange zest

Using a funnel, pour the Suze, Lillet, and gin into a 187-ml bottle. Top with the club soda, add the twist, and cap the bottle.

5. Pomegranate Fizz

HOMEMADE GRENADINE
MAKES ABOUT ½ CUP

½ cup pomegranate juice
½ cup sugar
1 tablespoon pomegranate molasses

MOCKTAIL

1 ounce Homemade Grenadine
6 ounces club soda
1 twist of lime zest

1. To make the grenadine: Bring the pomegranate juice, sugar, and pomegranate molasses to a boil in a small pan, stirring to dissolve the sugar. Remove the pan from the heat when the syrup is clear. Pour it into a glass jar, or through a funnel into a glass bottle, and cool to room temperature. This recipe makes enough for 8 cocktails. Cover and refrigerate for up to 1 month to reuse in this recipe, or try it in a Singapore Sling or Planter's Punch.

2. To make the Pomegranate Fizz: Using a funnel, pour the grenadine into a 187-ml bottle. Top with the club soda, add the twist, and cap the bottle.

Tips & Tricks:

Bottled Cocktails 101

Most of your favorite cocktails can be bottled, and besides being just plain fun, D.I.Y. bottling is a decidedly practical means of portioning, transporting, and serving drinks on the go. Purchase an inexpensive bottle capper, bottle caps, and mini Champagne bottles (see Picnic Provisions on page 185), and in mere minutes you'll have a bevy of bubblers ready to slip into the cooler. It's as easy as 1-2-3.

1. Prepare cocktails in individual bottles using a small funnel.
2. Place a cap on top of the bottle and seal with a Red Baron bottle capper. Invert the bottle to make sure you have a great seal.
3. Ice, pop, and sip!

EXTRA CREDIT

Order bottle caps that are painted on both sides for a prettier look. Or take advantage of inexpensive custom bottle cap production (see page 185 for retailers) so you can design your own for a one-of-a-kind tipple-topper.

Strawberry Shrub Sparkler

You can certainly break out this tart drinking vinegar after twenty-four hours, but it's even better after it mellows for a week, or two, or even all of July. Whenever you fancy a fast refresher, spoon a tablespoon or two of shrub into a glass and top with soda water. Return the shrub to the refrigerator and let it continue to evolve.

SERVES 6

1 cup Strawberry Shrub (recipe follows)
5 cups club soda
1 cup sliced strawberries
6 fresh mint sprigs

At the picnic site, mix the shrub, club soda, and strawberries in a pitcher. Pour into glasses of ice and garnish with a mint sprig.

IN THE BASKET:

- ☐ **Pitcher + wooden spoon**
- ☐ **Ice**
- ☐ **Glasses**
- ☐ **Paper straws**

Strawberry Shrub

MAKES ABOUT 1 CUP

1 cup sliced strawberries
1 cup granulated sugar
1 cup Champagne vinegar or white wine vinegar

TINY TIP: Reserve the muddled fruit, squeeze in the juice of half a lemon to balance the sweetness, and use it as an ice cream topping.

Combine the strawberries and sugar in a 1-quart Mason jar, cover, and refrigerate for 24 hours. Muddle the fruit with a wooden spoon whenever you think of it, at least four times. Strain the liquid through a fine-mesh strainer into a measuring cup (see Tiny Tip), then transfer it back to the jar and add the vinegar. Replace the lid and shake. Leave your shrub to mellow for at least 24 hours in the refrigerator, or up to 1 month.

The Basics of Brewing Iced Tea

While sun tea is romantic and cold-brewed tea trendy, there's only one way to make iced tea that's guaranteed to be both food-safe and ready in time for your picnic. Make a concentrated hot tea and pour it over ice for a result that's perfectly balanced every time. Here's how: Bring 8 cups water to a boil, then let it stand off the heat until it's 180°F, or about 5 minutes. Measure ¼ cup of loose-leaf tea directly into a large container, or into a large tea infuser, and pour the hot water over it. Steep according to the directions on the tea box, or simply follow your taste buds—the stronger and more tannic you prefer the tea, the longer it should steep. Most teas average a steeping time of 3 to 5 minutes. (Beware of overdoing it, as tea becomes bitter if left to infuse too long.) While the tea is steeping, fill your pitcher or beverage dispenser with 8 cups of ice, then pour your tea directly over the ice. (If the tea is floating loose in the water, strain it through a fine-mesh sieve.)

Tea-rithmetic

Use these simple teas, brewed as instructed in the "how-to" (see opposite page), and add all the trimmings, or experiment with blends. Just mix in any liquid sweetener (syrup or honey) before you pour the hot, freshly brewed tea over ice, and add other ingredients—like fruit, herbs, and spices—after the tea is fully chilled. Bring a cooler of ice to the picnic to fill glasses, and pour in the tea to serve it super cold. Each batch of the following flavored teas makes approximately 3 quarts.

A Whole New Pearl

To jasmine pearl tea, add 8 sprigs of fresh lavender.

Sen-cha-cha-cha

To sencha tea, add ½ English cucumber, thinly sliced, and three 8-inch stalks of lemongrass, sliced vertically and bruised with the side of a chef's knife.

Shiso Pretty

To genmaicha tea, add 3 ripe plums, thinly sliced, and ¼ cup fresh shiso leaves.

Vanilla-Peach Sweet Tea

To Ceylon tea, add ¼ cup Vanilla Bean Simple Syrup (page 168), 1 spent vanilla bean, and 1 peach, thinly sliced.

Triple Mint

To peppermint tea, add ¼ cup Mint Simple Syrup (page 169), 1 bunch fresh mint, and 1 cup fresh raspberries.

Red Tea at Night . . . Picnicker's Delight

To rooibos tea, add 1 tablespoon honey, 1 orange, thinly sliced into rounds, and 3 cinnamon sticks.

Sweet Valley Hi-biscus

To hibiscus tea, add syrup and flowers from half of an 8.8-ounce jar of Wild Hibiscus Flowers in Syrup.

Sticky Rice Is Really Nice

To pu-erh tea, add half a mango, thinly sliced.

Garden in a Glass

To white peony tea, add 8 sprigs chervil or parsley and a handful of pansies.

Can't Go Wrong Oolong

To oolong tea, add 1 nectarine, thinly sliced, and 3 star anise pods.

Six Simple Syrups

To add a touch of sweetness to any picnic sip, while avoiding sugar sediment at the bottom of the glass, make a homemade simple syrup. Each recipe makes ½ cup simple syrup. It'll keep in the fridge for one month. For easy use, store it in a squeeze bottle, but any covered container will do.

1. The Simplest Simple Syrup

½ cup sugar

½ cup water

Bring the sugar and water to a gentle simmer in a small pot. Stir frequently until the sugar has dissolved and the syrup is clear. Remove from heat and let stand to cool.

2. Vanilla Bean Simple Syrup

½ cup sugar

½ cup water

1 vanilla bean, split and seeded

Bring the sugar and water to a gentle simmer in a small pot. Stir frequently until the sugar has dissolved and the syrup is clear. Add the vanilla bean and continue to simmer for 5 minutes. Remove from heat and let stand to cool. Pour into a jar with the vanilla bean.

3. Lemon Simple Syrup

½ cup sugar

½ cup water

1 small lemon, zested with a peeler into ½-inch strips

Bring the sugar and water to a gentle simmer in a small pot. Stir frequently until the sugar has dissolved and the syrup is clear. Remove from the heat and add the lemon peel. Let the syrup steep for 1 hour. Strain the syrup into a jar. Reserve the lemon peel for garnish.

4. Mint Simple Syrup

½ cup sugar

½ cup water

1 cup loosely packed fresh mint

Bring the sugar and water to a gentle simmer in a small pot. Stir frequently until the sugar has dissolved and the syrup is clear. Remove from the heat and add the mint. Let the syrup steep for 1 hour. Strain the syrup into a jar.

5. Rosemary Simple Syrup

½ cup water

½ cup sugar

3 fresh rosemary sprigs

Bring the sugar and water to a gentle simmer in a small pot. Stir frequently until the sugar has dissolved and the syrup is clear. Remove from the heat and add the rosemary. Let the syrup steep for 1 hour. Strain the syrup into a jar.

6. Basil Simple Syrup

½ cup water

½ cup sugar

1 cup fresh basil leaves

Bring the sugar and water to a gentle simmer in a small pot. Stir frequently until the sugar has dissolved and the syrup is clear. Remove from the heat and add the basil. Let the syrup steep for 1 hour. Strain the syrup into a jar.

Mango-Cucumber Lassi

This minty mango and cucumber smoothie is inspired by a backpacking trip through Southeast Asia, where yogurt-based sippers are a highlight of any scorching day. Stateside, lassis are a refreshing counterpoint to spicy picnic fare. Even if you're having a picnic for two, whip up the whole batch—lassis are brilliant for breakfast.

MAKES 6

- 3 mangoes, peeled, pitted, and coarsely chopped
- 1 small cucumber, peeled and coarsely chopped
- 1 cup plain yogurt
- ½ cup milk
- 1 cup ice
- ¼ cup loosely packed fresh mint leaves

Blend the mangoes, cucumber, yogurt, milk, ice, and mint in a blender on high speed until smooth and creamy. Pour into six tall, 8-ounce Mason jars, screw on the lids, and chill for up to 2 days. Pack in a cooler to transport to the picnic. Lassis will keep for 2 days in the refrigerator.

IN THE BASKET:

- ☐ Straws

Raspberry Lemonade

The only thing nicer than icy cold lemonade on a hot day is icy cold *pink* lemonade on a hot day—adding puréed fresh raspberries gives it a strikingly picturesque pick-me-up. (You can substitute strawberries for the raspberries, if you like.) If Meyer lemons aren't abundant in your neck of the woods, regular lemon juice also works well but may require a bit more simple syrup. Taste as you go.

MAKES ABOUT 1½ QUARTS

4 cups fresh raspberries
1 cup fresh Meyer lemon juice
⅔ cup Lemon Simple Syrup (page 168)
3 cups still or sparkling water

Purée the raspberries on high speed in a blender or in a food processor. Pour the purée through a fine-mesh sieve to remove the seeds; you should have 1 cup of seedless raspberry purée. Pour it into a large pitcher, 2-quart Mason jar, or beverage dispenser and stir in the lemon juice, simple syrup, and water. At the picnic, add ice and serve.

IN THE BASKET:

- ☐ **Ice**
- ☐ **Glasses**

Watermelon Hibiscus Lime Agua Fresca

Aguas frescas translates to "fresh waters," and these traditional Mexican fruit drinks take their reputation seriously—nothing's quite as hydrating on a sweltering day, and since they're boozeless, you can drink as many cups as you want without having to retire early to your cabana. If you prefer your fruit water with a little sumpin' sumpin', however, just spike it with a splash of rum or tequila.

MAKES 10 CUPS

6 cups chopped seedless watermelon

6 cups water

One 8.8-ounce jar Wild Hibiscus Flowers in Syrup (available at specialty grocery stores)

2 limes, thinly sliced

¼ cup fresh lime juice, from 2 limes

IN THE BASKET:

- ☐ **Ice**
- ☐ **Glasses**
- ☐ **Spoon for stirring**
- ☐ **Wild Hibiscus Flowers in Syrup**

Purée the watermelon in a blender, then pour it through a fine-mesh strainer into a 2-quart lidded jar. Stir in the water, hibiscus syrup and flowers, lime slices, and lime juice. Secure the lid and pack the jar in a cooler with ice. At the picnic, shake the jar before serving the agua fresca over ice and garnish each drink with a hibiscus flower. Bring along a spoon to stir the mixture; it tends to separate over time.

Elderflower Pimm's Cup

Is there anything better than a summer sipper that contains a sizeable snack? You'll like this light spirit just as much as its pretty accompaniments. Pack your cooler with individual cocktails for a delicious, cheerful refreshment.

SERVES 1

2 ounces Pimm's No. 1 Cup
1 ounce St. Germain liqueur
1 tablespoon fresh lemon juice
1 tablespoon Lemon Simple Syrup (page 168)
1 strawberry, hulled and quartered
1 thin slice orange, quartered
3 thin slices cucumber
Club soda
1 mint sprig
1½ strips lemon peel, from Lemon Simple Syrup

Combine the booze, lemon juice, and simple syrup in a Mason jar. Add the strawberry, orange, and cucumber. Replace the lid and pack in a cooler filled with ice. At the picnic, add ice, top with club soda, garnish with a mint sprig and lemon peel strip, add a straw, and serve.

IN THE BASKET:

- ☐ **Mint sprigs**
- ☐ **Paper straws**
- ☐ **Ice**
- ☐ **Club soda**

Menu: Piñata Party

Book the mariachi band, dust the tortilla chip crumbs off your sombrero, and perfect your "Olé!"

Tortilla Chips, Salsa, and Guacamole

Cabbage, Pineapple, and Spiced Pepita Slaw 86

Horseradish-Rubbed Flank Steak with Blistered Tomatoes (served with tortillas) 112

Fresh-Fruit Paletas 132

Watermelon Hibiscus Lime Agua Fresca 172

Spicy Paloma Punch 175

Spicy Paloma Punch

While margaritas swing from overly sweet to undeniably superb, the Paloma never fails to delight. Mix fresh grapefruit juice with serrano peppers and tequila for a classy one-two punch. Add a sweet scoop of sorbet to each cup—it'll cool the drink and freshen it as it melts.

SERVES 6 TO 8

- 1 bottle cava
- 4 cups fresh grapefruit juice (from about 5 large grapefruits)
- 2 cups reposado tequila
- ½ cup fresh lime juice
- ¼ cup Simplest Simple Syrup (page 168)
- 1 small pink grapefruit, thinly sliced
- 1 serrano chile, thinly sliced
- 1 pint lemon sorbet

Mix the cava, grapefruit juice, tequila, lime juice, and simple syrup in a beverage dispenser. Garnish with the slices of grapefruit and chile. At the picnic, place a scoop of lemon sorbet in each cup and pour in the punch.

IN THE BASKET:

- ☐ **Punch cups**
- ☐ **Sorbet + ice cream scoop**
- ☐ **Punch bowl + ladle**

Sour Cherry Sangria

This Spanish sangria marries stone fruit and bright red sour cherries (aka pie cherries) with vinho verde, an inexpensive, slightly effervescent Portuguese white wine that's perfect for a fruit-forward punch. The pucker of the plums and sweetness of the nectarines play off the tart cherries nicely, but any mixture of stone fruit will do. If you're serving a smaller party, simply cut this recipe in half.

SERVES 6 TO 8

2 cups sour cherries, pitted
4 plums, pitted and sliced
2 nectarines, pitted and sliced
8 thyme sprigs
½ cup brandy
¼ cup Simplest of Simple Syrups (page 168)
2 bottles vinho verde

Place the cherries, plums, nectarines, and thyme in the bottom of a large pitcher or a 2-quart glass jar. Add the brandy, simple syrup, and vinho verde and stir to combine. Cover the sangria and chill in the refrigerator for at least 4 hours, preferably overnight. At the picnic, stir the sangria before serving over ice.

IN THE BASKET:

- ☐ **Long spoon for stirring**
- ☐ **Stemless wineglasses**
- ☐ **Ice**

Mint Juleps en Masse

Truth be told, we love any cocktail en masse, but mint juleps lend themselves particularly well to being prepared by the bunch. This batched cocktail swaps the muddled mint with mint-infused simple syrup. Serve the juleps over crushed ice in pewter cups, garnish with mint, and you're off to the races. Or consider bottling the juleps individually (see instructions on page 164).

SERVES 6

½ cup Mint Simple Syrup (page 169)
2 cups Maker's Mark bourbon whisky
Crushed ice (see Tiny Tip)
Fresh mint sprigs

Stir together the simple syrup and whisky in a 2-quart glass jar. Pack the jar, ice, and mint in a cooler. At the picnic, fill glasses with ice, pour in the cocktail, and garnish each with a sprig of mint.

IN THE BASKET:

- ☐ Crushed ice
- ☐ Cups (bonus points if they're pewter)
- ☐ Fresh mint garnish

TINY TIP: Buy a bag of crushed ice at the store, or place ice cubes in a resealable plastic bag and have at it with a rolling pin or meat mallet—with apologies to your downstairs neighbors.

The Portland

A nod to our hometown's notoriously moody winter weather (which is one of the reasons we worship the onset of picnic season so enthusiastically), this rendition of the classic Dark and Stormy cocktail is made with black rum. Its rich molasses flavor is the perfect foil for gingery liqueur and zingy lime juice. Mix the first three ingredients in a Mason jar and top with ginger beer once you arrive at the picnic.

SERVES 6

8 ounces Cruzan Black Strap Rum

8 ounces Domaine de Canton ginger liqueur

⅓ cup fresh lime juice

Ice

One 6-pack ginger beer

1 lime, cut into 6 wedges

Mix the rum, Domaine de Canton, and lime juice in a Mason jar or bottle and take it to the picnic. On the blanket, fill tall 8-ounce glasses or jars with ice and pour 3 ounces of the cocktail base into each, top with ginger beer, and serve with a lime wedge.

IN THE BASKET:

- ☐ **Ice**
- ☐ **Tumblers**
- ☐ **Ginger beer**
- ☐ **Lime wedges**

Three Peerless Picnic Beers

For a simple summer refresher, stock up on great craft beer. We turn to our picnic partner, beer writer Lucy Burningham, to tell us exactly how to pick a winner.

When choosing the right beer for your picnic, think light and versatile. Beers with lighter body, lots of bubbles, and a refreshing crispness will pair well with almost any picnic fare. Also, beers with less alcohol will let you sip for longer. A "sessionable" beer, one you can drink for a long session, has less than 5 percent alcohol by volume (ABV) and lends itself to hot summer days. These three types of beer are notably picnic perfect.

1. Fruit Beers

These beers capture the essence of summer by showcasing flavors of seasonal fruit. Styles can range from light wheat beers to Belgian strong ales, so be wary of fruit beers that are too heavy-handed. Some are fermented with real fruit—peaches, cherries, pears, or raspberries—which can add a delicious layer of freshness to the beer.

2. Saisons

Originally brewed in Belgian and French farmhouses, these ales are complex thanks to their yeasts, which can come off as rich and earthy. Ideal for pairing with food, the best saisons are highly carbonated and may have fruity or citrusy notes. Consider tartness a bonus.

3. Pilsners

A classic German-style lager, primo pilsners have crackery flavors that come from the Pils malt, a bit of spiciness from traditional hops, and a dry crispness that pairs well with everything from spicy foods to creamy desserts.

TINY TIP

To serve your sips cold, assign one friend ice duty. Ask her to line her picnic basket with a plastic bag and fill it with ice. Flip open the lid for an instant wine or beer cooler.

Drink Pink: Four Tips for Buying Rosé

From demure Willamette Valley beauties the color of peony petals to vibrant apricot-hued Corsican vintages, here's how to pick the perfect pink.

1. Bandol Knows Best

The Provençal region of Bandol produces some of the finest rosés ever sipped. To pick a winning bottle every time, look for these producers: Tempier, Pibarnon, Gros' Noré, Terrebrune, and Pradeaux. Or sail southeast—Corsica is rising in rosé stardom.

2. The Price Is Right

Rosé is surprisingly affordable despite its elegant air, and you really needn't spend more than $15 to show up with a crowd-pleaser.

3. Don't Be Ageist

Unlike red wine, rosé is meant to be drunk young (in most cases), so don't shy away from trying a label's current vintage. Once you find a bottle you like, stock up for the summer with a case.

4. Practice Makes Perfect

Never has trial and error been more painless. Opt for the rosé flight at your favorite wine bar, ask the best sommeliers in town what they drink, or subscribe to your favorite bottle shop's newsletter to stay up on rosé tastings. Soon, you'll be buying rosé like a natural-born Parisian.

Wine Key 911

In the tragic event of a forgotten corkscrew, do not lose hope. A savvy picnicker is infinitely resourceful. (Remove the foil before attempting any of the following.)

- Saber off the top of the bottle with the chef's knife you brought to slice dessert. (Professional training required.)
- Twist a corn-on-the-cob holder into the cork, pull, and pray.
- Assuming you have your toolbox at the ready, drive a screw partway into the cork and then pull it out with pliers.
- Pierce the cork with a knife to release the pressure and then push the cork into the bottle with the end of a serving spoon.
- Select a tree (preferably one with soft bark to cushion the blow) and hit the bottom of the wine bottle against its trunk repeatedly. After a minute or so, the cork will be forced out. (Seriously, this works!) Just in case you don't know your own strength, wrap a towel around the wine bottle to protect your hand against accidental breakage.
- Call an understanding significant other.

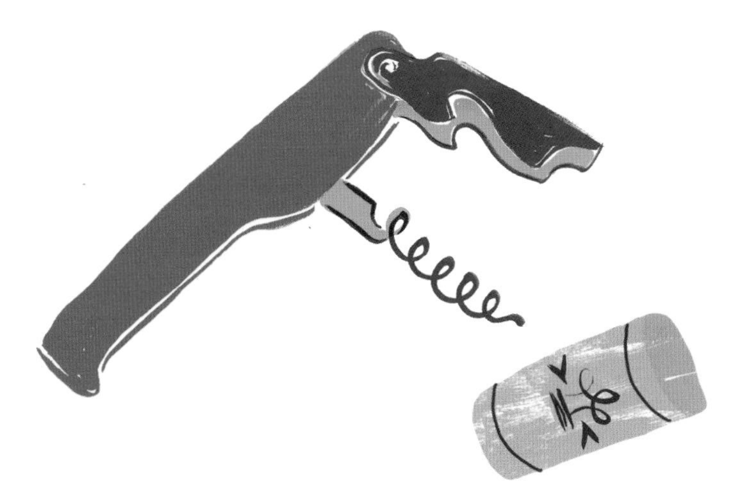

How to Host a Rosé Rumble

Even the most stalwart sipper would find opening a dozen bottles in one sitting overwhelming, so gather a group for a pink wine showdown.

1. Challenge guests to bring their most highly regarded rosé and a wineglass to a French-themed garden picnic. (See Dueling French Picnics, page 154.)
2. Set the scene with bunches of fresh lavender, cocktail napkins stamped with fleurs-de-lis, tiny Alma Chocolate frogs, and a portable speaker crooning Edith Piaf. Prepare a selection of snacks from the Picnic in Provence menu (page 154).
3. As picnickers arrive proudly bearing their selection, slip each bottle into a paper lunch sack. Tie a piece of twine around the bottle's neck and attach a pen.
4. Instruct the guests to pass around each contender, pour a taste, and write their tasting notes on the bag.
5. When the evening winds down, read the tasting notes, tally up the glowing reviews, and declare a winner.

Tasting Tips

Not sure how to express your feelings when drinking rosé? Mix and match these insider terms to create thoughtful tasting notes that will leave people certain of your wine savvy.

"This rosé is a beautiful shade of . . . "	"I taste . . . "	"Hmm, that's very . . . "
Blush	Wild strawberries	Tart
Salmon	Grapefruit	Dry
Carnation	Dried apple	Sweet
Rose	Rose petals	Earthy
Magenta	Blood orange	Tangy
Coral	Apricot	Floral
Ruby	Peach	Crisp
Fuchsia	Honeysuckle	Juicy
Mauve	Tangerine	Bright
Berry	Red currant	Nervy
Cranberry	Pomegranate	Luscious
Barbie Dreamhouse	Cherry Jolly Ranchers	Fruit-driven
	Grapes	Wet

Until We Picnic Again

At the end of the summer, we'd do anything to extend picnic season—be that trade our baskets for backpacks and set out on a hiking picnic, organize a caravan to California for one last wine country picnic, or bundle up in down jackets for a chilly snowshoe picnic. Eventually, and reluctantly, we accept that summer has ended and we'll just have to wait another year for peaches so juicy they drip down your arm as you slice them, raspberries so ripe you want to eat them by the pint, and iced tea so refreshing you'll brew pitcher after pitcher of it.

When it's time to settle into the cozy season of baking and comfort cooking, our minds drift to picnics past. And, in recalling the meals we ate, the places we sat, and the company we kept, we're instantly transported to sunshine-drenched days of summer. Because it's recalling what made us laugh, and kept us up late, and had us licking our plates that keeps us smiling all year round. We wish you a lifetime of marvelous picnics, and even more than that, we wish you the kind of friends who make picnicking such a delight.

PICNIC PROVISIONS

Fantastic Food and Drink

Alma Chocolate
www.almachocolate.com
Fine bonbons and seasonal molded chocolates.

The Brooklyn Larder
www.bklynlarder.com
Picnic heaven: a surfeit of specialty ingredients like colatura, Ortiz tuna, and piment d'Espelette.

Cheese Bar
www.cheese-bar.com
A spot-on selection of cheeses curated by the Cheese Whisperer.

Cowgirl Creamery
www.cowgirlcreamery.com
A truly exceptional assortment of cheeses.

Murray's Cheese
www.murrayscheese.com
Cheese, charcuterie, and accoutrements.

Olympic Provisions
www.olympicprovisions.com
Old-world style salami, pâté, rillettes, and pickled vegetables.

Russ and Daughters
www.russanddaughters.com
Smoked fish, caviar, and dried fruit.

Steven Smith Teamaker
www.smithtea.com
Tip-top teas straight from the expert.

The Meadow
www.atthemeadow.com
Artisan salts, chocolates, and bitters.

Quin
www.quincandy.com
Gumdrops and other sweet goodies from Portland's premier candy shop.

Xocolatl de Davíd
www.xocolatldedavid.com
Creatively flavored chocolate bars.

Zingerman's
www.zingermans.com
Any picnic sundry you could ever need, delivered to your door.

Baskets, Blankets, and Beyond

Anthropologie
www.anthropologie.com
We tip our picnic hats to the retailer that's as obsessed with stylish picnics as we are, offering picnic totes, deviled egg plates, and sunshine attire.

Bambu
www.bambuhome.com
Bamboo plates and serveware.

Best Buy
www.bestbuy.com
Projector for an outdoor movie night.

Bottle Cap Company
www.bottlecapco.com
Bottle caps galore, even customizable ones.

CB2
www.cb2.com
Transport gear, melamine plates, utensils.

Crate & Barrel
www.crateandbarrel.com
Baskets, picnic coolers, wooden flatware, wineglass holders.

Fortnum & Mason
www.fortnumandmason.com
Opulent, inspiring formal picnic hampers.

Home Brewing
www.homebrewing.com
Bottled cocktail paraphernalia: Red Baron bottle capper, 7-ounce glass bottles, bottle caps.

IKEA
www.ikea.com
French lemonade bottles and inexpensive picnic gear.

Jaques America
www.jaquesamerica.com
Every sort of lawn game.

J. K. Adams Co.
www.jkadams.com
Vermont-made cutting boards of all shapes and sizes.

Kate Spade
www.katespade.com
Outdoor tableware and the one-and-only Champagne Picnic Basket.

Kaufmann Mercantile
www.kaufmann-mercantile.com
Enamel food containers and quality outdoor gear.

Le Parfait
www.leparfait.com
Fabulously French hinge-top jars.

L. L. Bean
www.llbean.com
Classic lawn games, portable fire pits.

Nordstrom
shop.nordstrom.com
Linens, totes, and, perhaps most important, the prettiest picnic attire and shoes.

Opinel
www.opinel-usa.com
Well-priced, elegant folding knives.

Paper Source
www.paper-source.com
Gable boxes, favor bags, and menus.

Paperless Post
www.paperlesspost.com
Delightful invitations, both virtual and snail.

Pendleton
www.pendleton-usa.com
Gorgeous patterned picnic blankets made in the Pacific Northwest.

Provisions by Food52
www.food52.com/provisions
Handwoven picnic baskets, outdoor serveware, linens, and Mason cocktail shakers.

Schoolhouse Electric
www.schoolhouseelectric.com
Enamel food containers, linen napkins, bottle openers.

Shop Sweet Lulu
www.shopsweetlulu.com
Pretty packaging, paper straws, paper baking pans.

Sur La Table
www.surlatable.com
Cheese signs, oyster knifes, and outdoor glassware.

Target
www.target.com
Everything. Particularly Pyrex baking dishes, Norpro ice-pop molds, and Stanley thermoses.

Weck Jars
www.weckjars.com
Exceptional jars.

West Elm
www.westelm.com
Colorful melamine platters, lanterns, linens.

Williams-Sonoma
www.williams-sonoma.com
Your one-stop picnic cookware shop.

Woolrich
www.woolrich.com
Wool picnic blankets made in the USA.

ACKNOWLEDGMENTS

We adore our editor, Judy Pray, without whom these recipes would have remained in our picnic baskets. Thank you for seeing what this book could be from the start, and for editing it with grace and humor. Many thanks to Sharon Bowers for finding our ideal publishing match. And hats off to Artisan for treating us with the extraordinary care so characteristic of the imprint, particularly Lelia Mander, Nancy Murray, and Lia Ronnen. Thank you to our right-hand gal, Mura Dominko; our clever designers, Michelle Ishay-Cohen and Renata Di Biase; and Emily Isabella, our illustrator soul mate, who somehow drew our picnic dreams right on paper.

A huge thank-you to the lovely Lila Martin, who helped make this book happen, and whose tireless attention to detail keeps the Portland Picnic Society in motion. And a magnum of rosé bubbly to the other gorgeous gals of our picnic club: Katie Burnett, Lucy Burningham, Michelle Cairo, Danielle Centoni, Brenda Crow, Sarah Curtis-Fawley, Cana Flug, Sarah Hart, Alexis Heimlich, Mona Johnson, Kristen Murray, Hannah Sullivan, and Califia Suntree.

Thank you to our mascot, Winnie; our energetic recipe testers, Jamie and Jeff; our original editorial enthusiasts, Miranda Jones and Molly Erman; and all of the chocolate bars that were harmed in the making of this book.

Finally, we would like to thank our families for taking us on our first picnics. They had no idea.

INDEX

Note: Page numbers followed by an **m** *refer to menus.*

CONVERSION CHARTS

Here are rounded-off equivalents between the metric system and the traditional systems that are used in the United States to measure weight and volume.

FRACTIONS	DECIMALS
⅛	.125
¼	.25
⅓	.33
⅜	.375
½	.5
⅝	.625
⅔	.67
¾	.75
⅞	.875

WEIGHTS

US/UK	METRIC
¼ oz	7 g
½ oz	15 g
1 oz	30 g
2 oz	55 g
3 oz	85 g
4 oz	110 g
5 oz	140 g
6 oz	170 g
7 oz	200 g
8 oz (½ lb)	225 g
9 oz	250 g
10 oz	280 g
11 oz	310 g
12 oz	340 g
13 oz	370 g
14 oz	400 g
15 oz	425 g
16 oz (1 lb)	455 g

VOLUME

AMERICAN	IMPERIAL	METRIC
¼ tsp		1.25 ml
½ tsp		2.5 ml
1 tsp		5 ml
½ Tbsp (1½ tsp)		7.5 ml
1 Tbsp (3 tsp)		15 ml
¼ cup (4 Tbsp)	2 fl oz	60 ml
L cup (5 Tbsp)	2½ fl oz	75 ml
½ cup (8 Tbsp)	4 fl oz	125 ml
M cup (10 Tbsp)	5 fl oz	150 ml
O cup (12 Tbsp)	6 fl oz	175 ml
1 cup (16 Tbsp)	8 fl oz	250 ml
1¼ cups	10 fl oz	300 ml
1½ cups	12 fl oz	350 ml
2 cups (1 pint)	16 fl oz	500 ml
2½ cups	20 fl oz (1 pint)	625 ml
5 cups	40 fl oz (1 qt)	1.25 l

OVEN TEMPERATURES

	°F	°C	GAS MARK
very cool	250–275	130–140	½–1
cool	300	148	2
warm	325	163	3
moderate	350	177	4
moderately hot	375–400	190–204	5–6
hot	425	218	7
very hot	450–475	232–245	8–9